LITTLE BOOK OF

miu miu

Published in 2025 by Welbeck
An Imprint of HEADLINE PUBLISHING GROUP LIMITED

1

Cataloguing in Publication Data is available from the British Library

ISBN 9781035420612

Printed in China

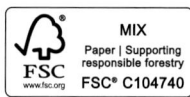

HEADLINE PUBLISHING GROUP LIMITED
An Hachette UK Company
Carmelite House
50 Victoria Embankment
London EC4Y 0DZ

The authorised representative in the EEA is Hachette Ireland,
8 Castlecourt Centre, Dublin 15, D15 XTP3, Ireland (email: info@hbgi.ie)

www.headline.co.uk
www.hachette.co.uk

LITTLE BOOK OF

miu miu

The story of the iconic fashion house

KRISTEN BATEMAN

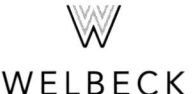

WELBECK

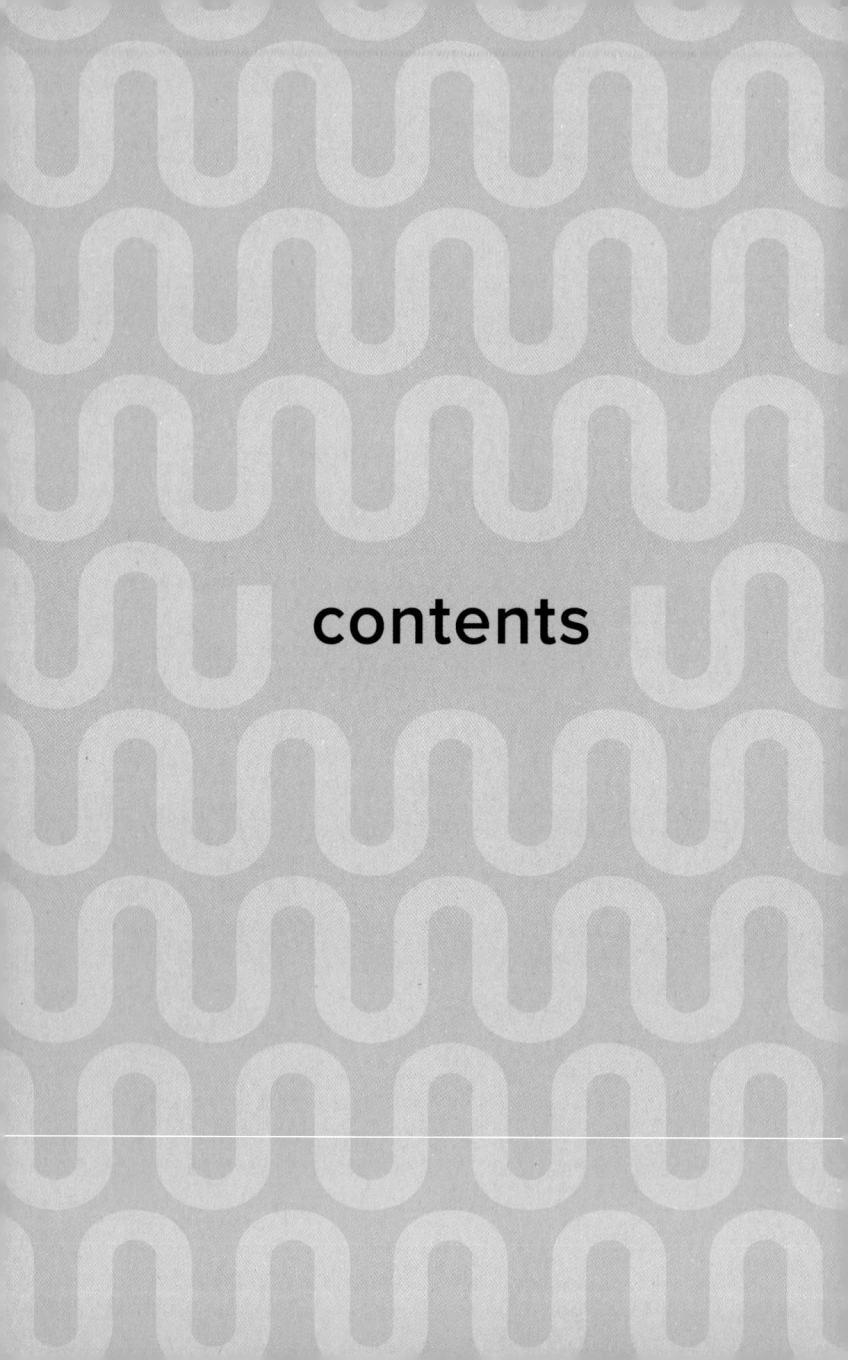

contents

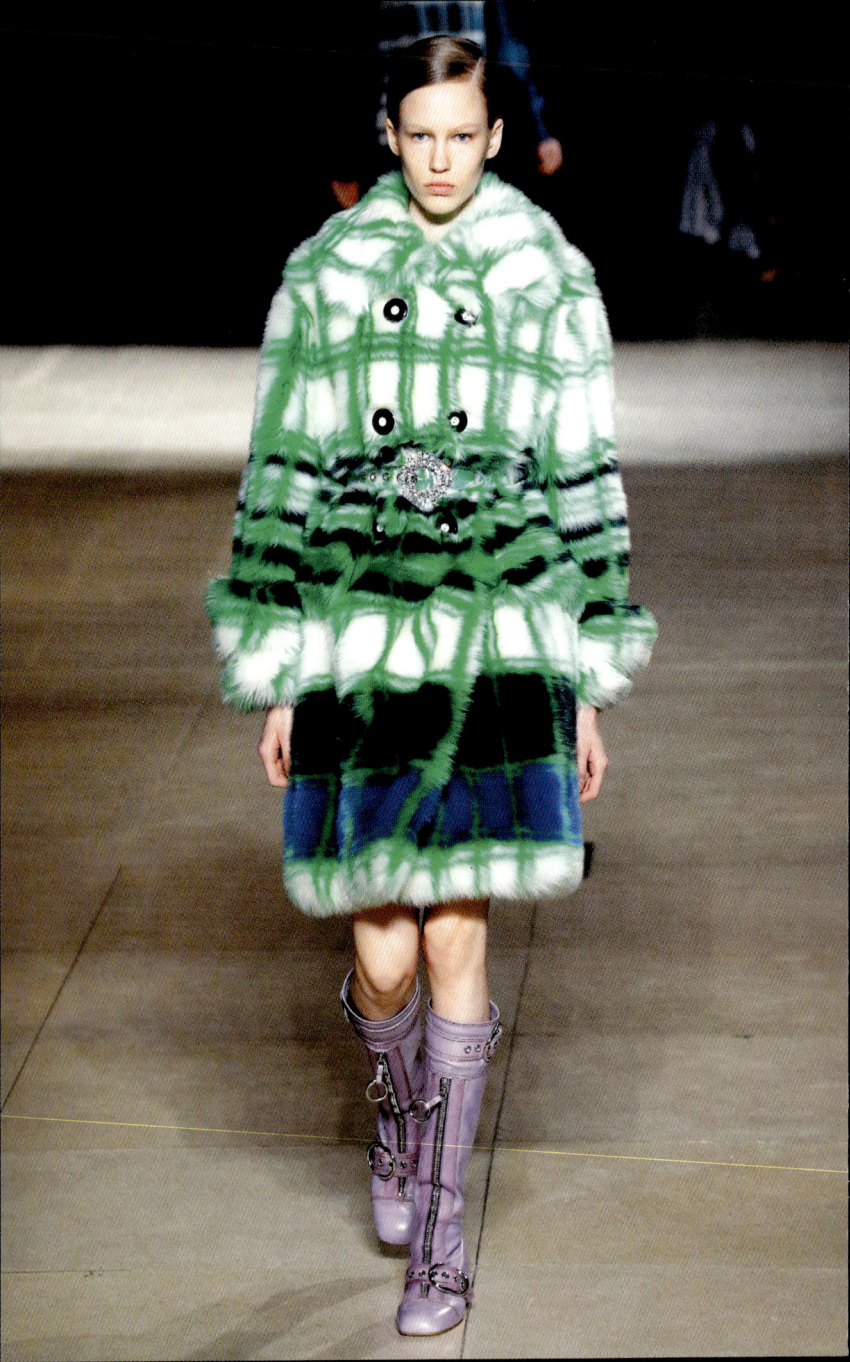

introduction

Miuccia Prada is one of the rare designers in the world of fashion with an irreplaceable point of view. Not only with Prada, but even more so with Miu Miu – long-heralded by the fashion industry as the little sister brand of Prada.

Cemented in the early days of the brand, and even more so in the mid 2010s, Miu Miu became the definitive brand designed for women from a woman's point of view. Think: quirky yet intellectual prints, off-kilter colours that don't usually go together, ingenious styling hacks, clothing presented in a way that makes you rethink everything, and just the right amount of accessories that speak volumes about Miuccia Prada's aesthetic and the deeper codes within the brand. "I'm always trying to do something that is never to please men in the most banal way," she told *Women's Wear Daily* (*WWD*).

When it comes to distilling the distinct aesthetic of the brand, Miu Miu, like many other brands, has seen different eras throughout the years. Perhaps most unique is the label's ability to move seamlessly between worlds. It began as a sort of minimalist anti-fashion brand and has seamlessly shifted from clean lines and utilitarian dressing with an injection of wit to mastering prints and colours through a distinctly feminine lens. It's now positioned itself as a brand that changes culture in an instant – from viral micro miniskirts and librarian chic glasses to neon peacoats with pearls and back again.

OPPOSITE A model wearing a maximalist faux fur coat for Miu Miu's Autumn/Winter 2017 runway show.

No other brand represents such a strong point of view, or offers such daring dressing, even through the vein of the most basic of wardrobe staples like a polo shirt or ballet flat. This book charts the history of Miu Miu and what it represents, from the iconic runway shows to all the hidden house codes, style muses, art collaborations and more.

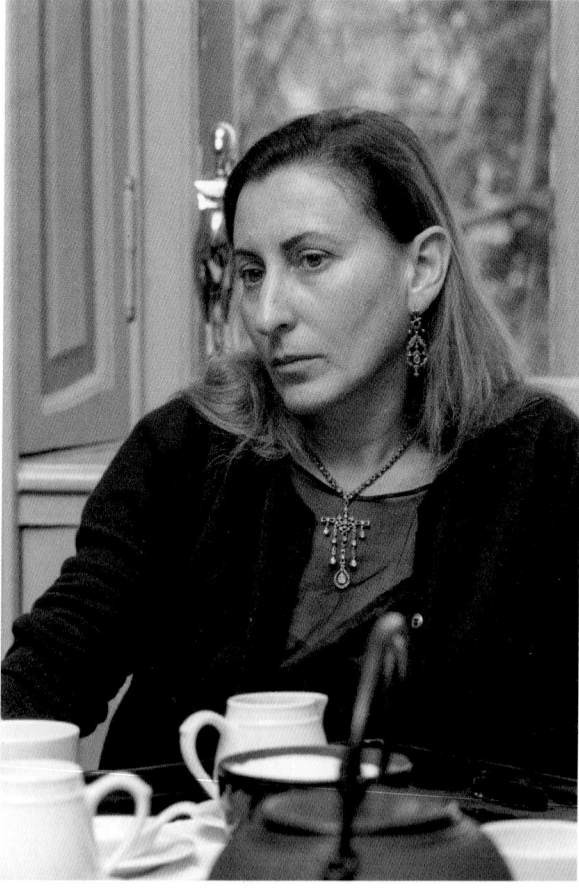

LEFT Miuccia Prada herself has been known to dress in her own sort of uniform, often with vintage jewellery.

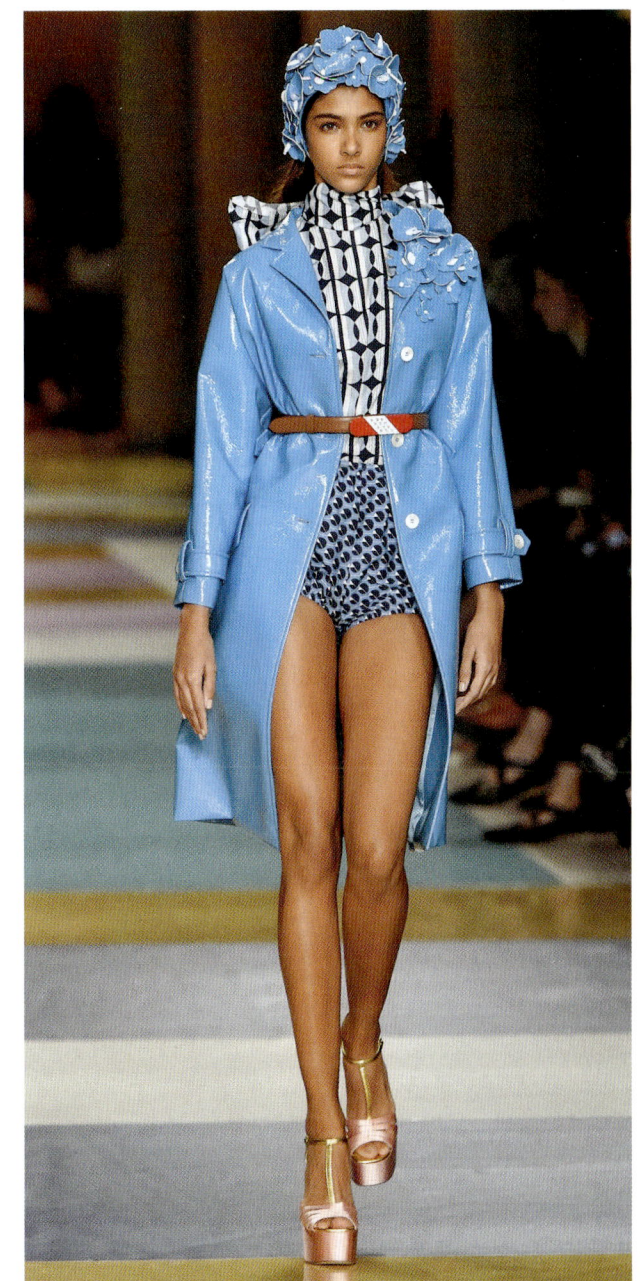

RIGHT The Spring/Summer 2017 collection experimented with vintage-inspired swimwear and presented iconic swim caps.

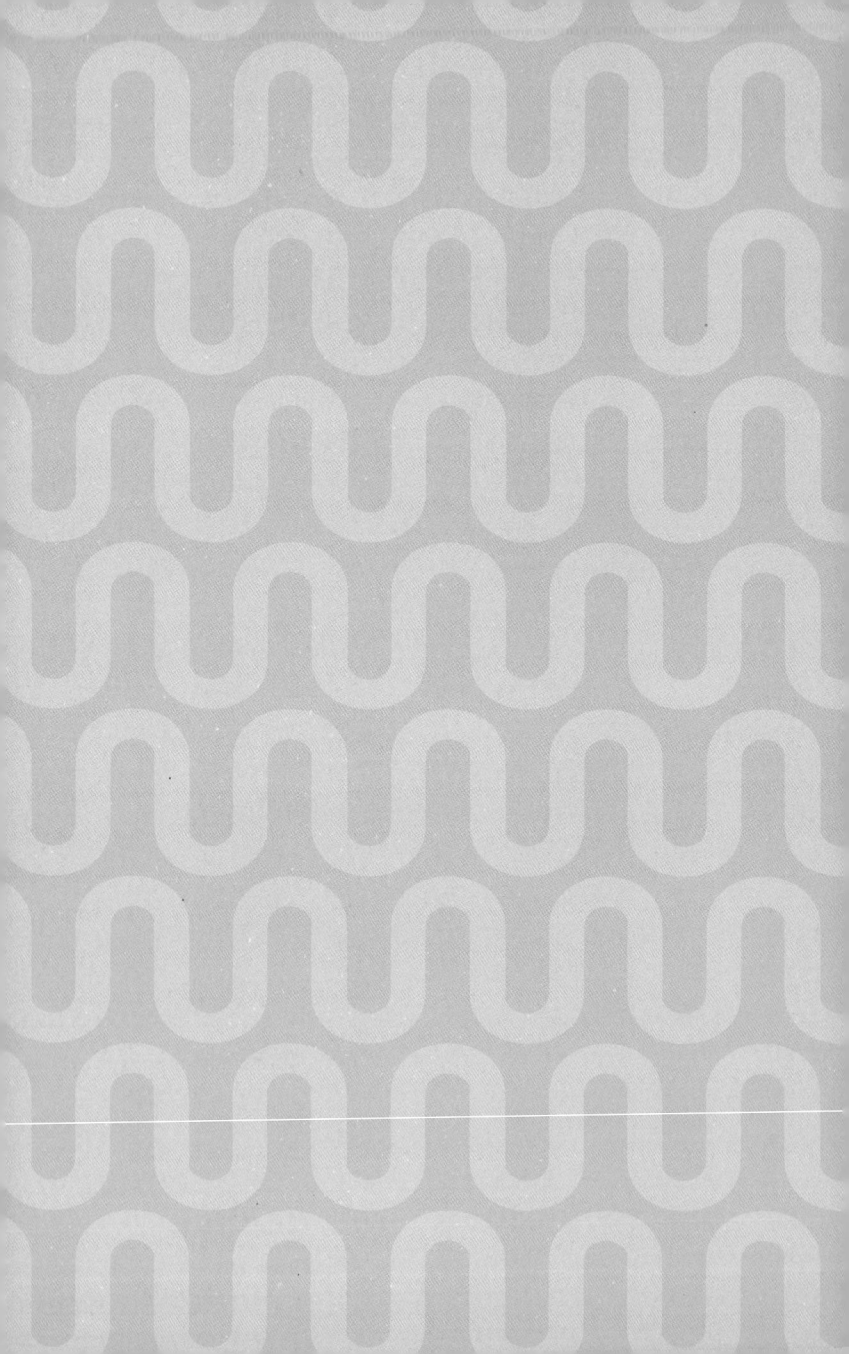

the making
of miu miu

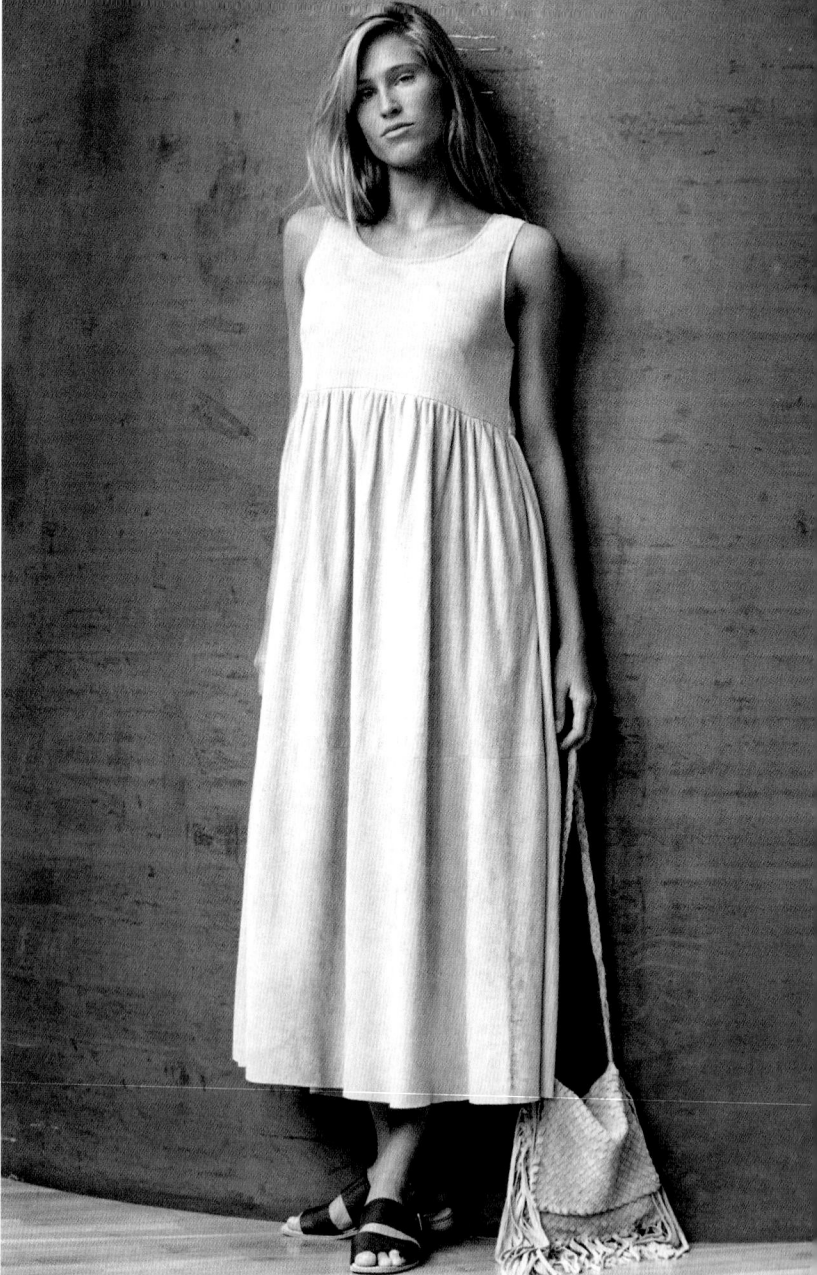

miu miu's beginnings

When Miuccia Prada, iconic titan of the fashion industry, launched Miu Miu in 1993, she created the brand as a platform of recklessly creative femininity. From the beginning, Miu Miu has always been designed for women from a woman's point of view. Call it the ultimate brand for the female gaze, if you will.

From Prada to Miu Miu

M iuccia Prada took the name "Miu Miu" from her own nickname. And although she's a legend today – known even to people who don't frequent the world of fashion – it wasn't always that way. In 1971, she graduated from the University of Milan with a PhD in political science while at the same time studying the art of mime at Milan's Piccolo Teatro. As a student, she was interested in politics, joining youth-led demonstrations and strikes in the late 1960s. She was also a member of the Union of Italian Women, a feminist collective of the Communist Party. And while many are intrigued by this fact, it wasn't all that uncommon for young Italians to be involved with that side of politics in the late '60s: "Every young kid who was vaguely clever was leftist, so it's not

OPPOSITE A look from one of Miu Miu's earliest collections, which channelled a bohemian free spirit.

that I was so special," she explained to *Document Journal* in 2015.

It was only in the late 1970s that she became globally known. As the youngest granddaughter of Mario Prada, Miuccia Prada took over the Prada brand in 1978. The same year, she met her husband and business partner, Patrizio Bertelli. He would go on to have a massive influence on the business side of Prada and Miu Miu, creating factories across Italy and strategizing on production, quality and retail.

Prada was known for its leathers, but even early on, Miuccia Prada instilled her quirky point of view, which later paved the way for similar concepts at Miu Miu. It was all about thinking differently. Take, for example, the iconic nylon Prada backpack that shocked the world in 1984. "Back then, I didn't really like anything I saw. It all just looked so old and bourgeois and boring. I just wanted to search for the absolute opposite of what was already out there," she told *Vogue*. "Suddenly, nylon started

BELOW Miu Miu has always had a strong point of view when it comes to footwear, which is why the brand's early shoes remain highly collectible on the second-hand market.

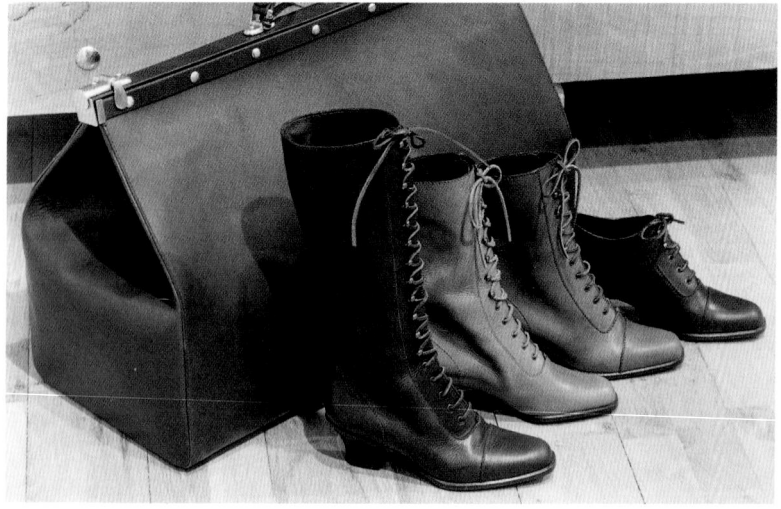

to look more intriguing to me than couture fabrics. I decided to introduce it to the catwalk, and it challenged, even changed, the traditional and conservative idea of luxury. I am still obsessed with it."

In 1988, four years after changing the course of fashion history with the nylon backpack, Miuccia Prada launched Prada's first ready-to-wear clothing collection. This decision confirmed her as an indelible force in fashion, known for her cutting-edge style, from bags to shoes and now dresses, trousers, blouses and every other fashion item under the sun. By the early 1990s, Prada was specializing in bold, minimalist utilitarian fashion, with quirky, feminine house codes. This all laid out the framework for Miu Miu – which was born in 1993.

The Autumn/Winter 1993 collection was Miu Miu's first. "Prada, at the end, is what I am, and Miu Miu is what I would like to be," Miuccia Prada famously said in 1997. Long shearling coats were paired with pony hair cow spot bags, while caramel-hued fur-trimmed fringe bags melded with knitted dresses with little ruffled hems. For footwear, there were sturdy leather boots and clogs. Patchwork suede maxi dresses, brown suede bags trimmed with shiny silver grommets and cow print clogs sealed the deal. The collection was released via a lookbook rather than through an extravagant runway show, and it was already clear that Miu Miu was a brand that played with the idea of taste and womanhood. In this collection alone, Miuccia Prada integrated elements of girlhood and adulthood, juxtaposed with aesthetics that weren't necessarily conventionally attractive.

"When I started, everybody hated what I was doing except a few clever people!" the designer told *Document Journal*. "Because it was not for the classic ones – there was something disturbing. And for the super trendy avant-gardists, it was too classic. I always like to move in that space, never please anybody."

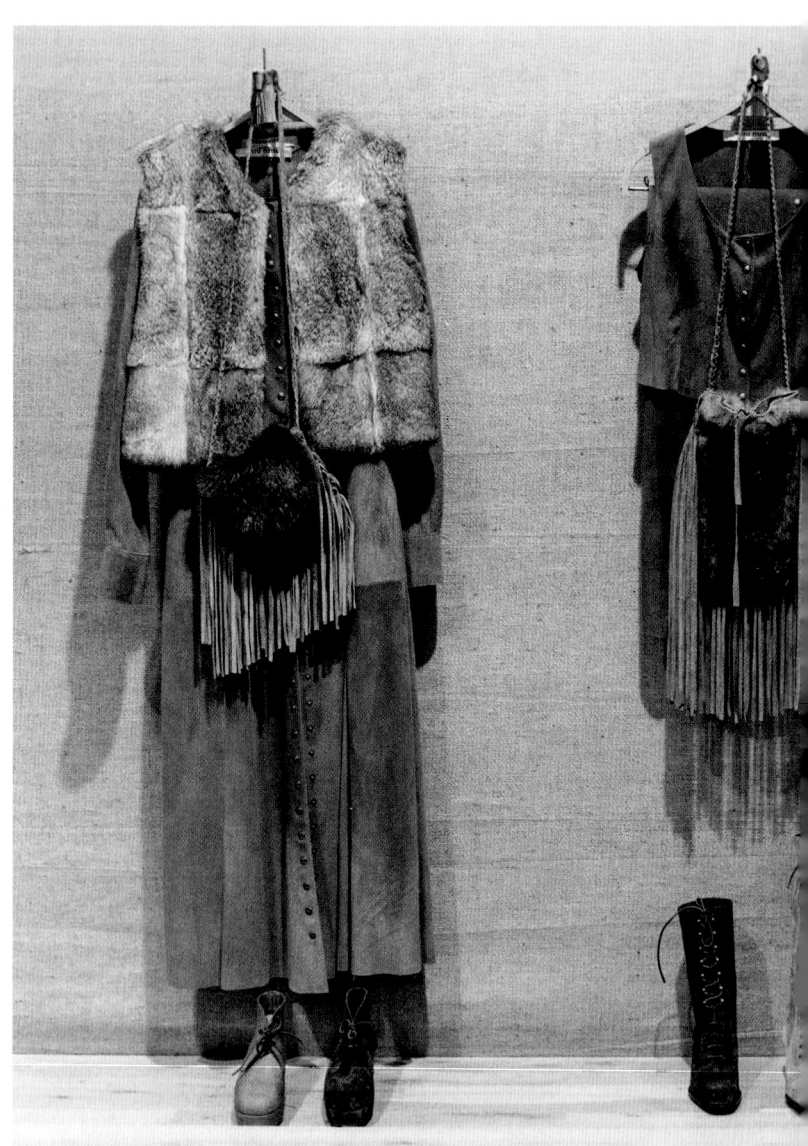

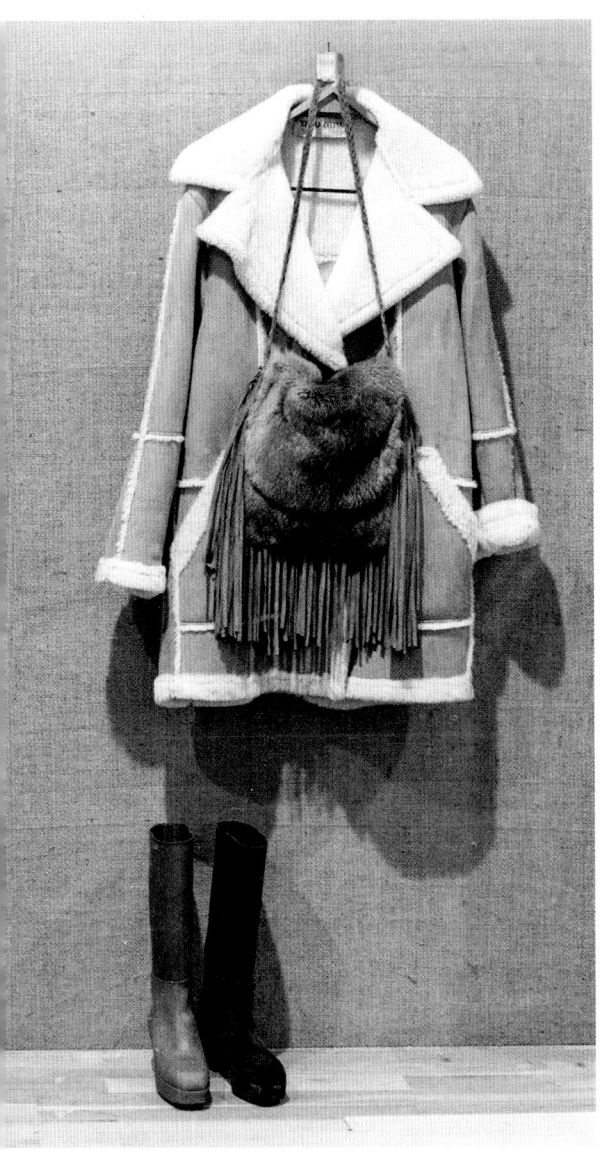

LEFT In the early days, Miu Miu mixed natural fabrics – suede, leather, shearling and cottons – for a distinct look.

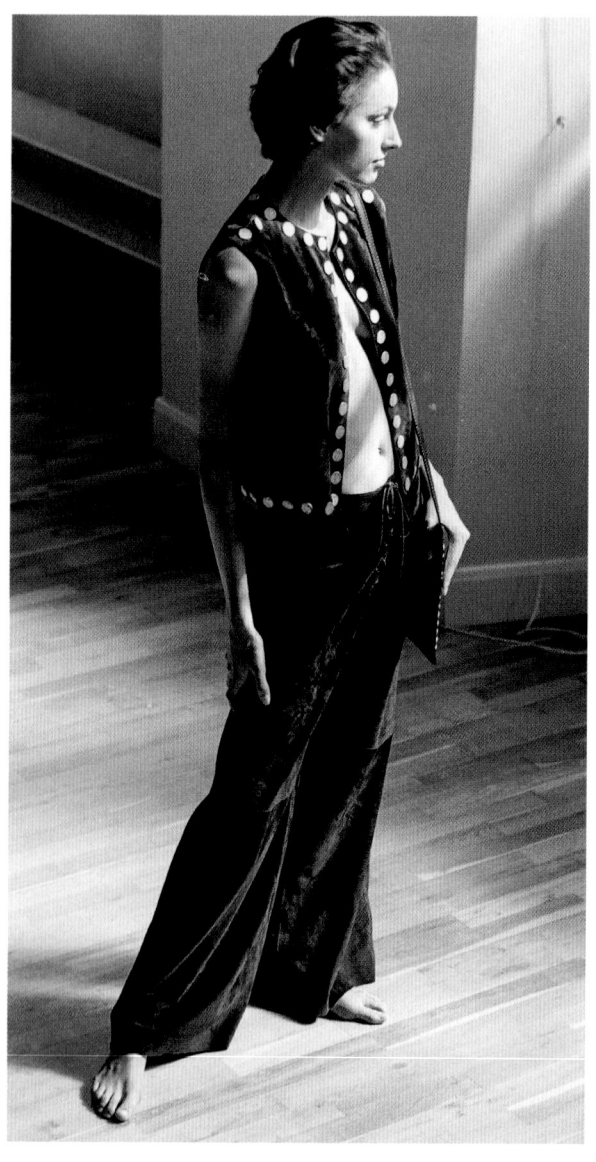

LEFT Miuccia Prada has always taken inspiration from past eras and decades, meshing them together to reinterpret them – as seen here.

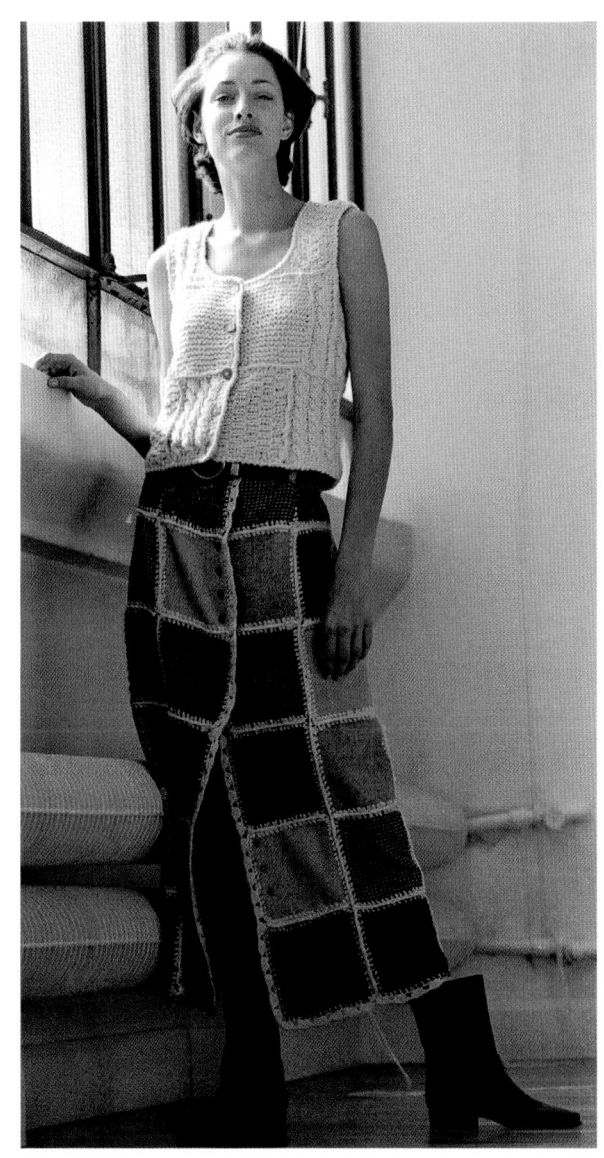

RIGHT An early example of a Miu Miu patchwork skirt and knitted top – both go-tos that the brand reworks again and again.

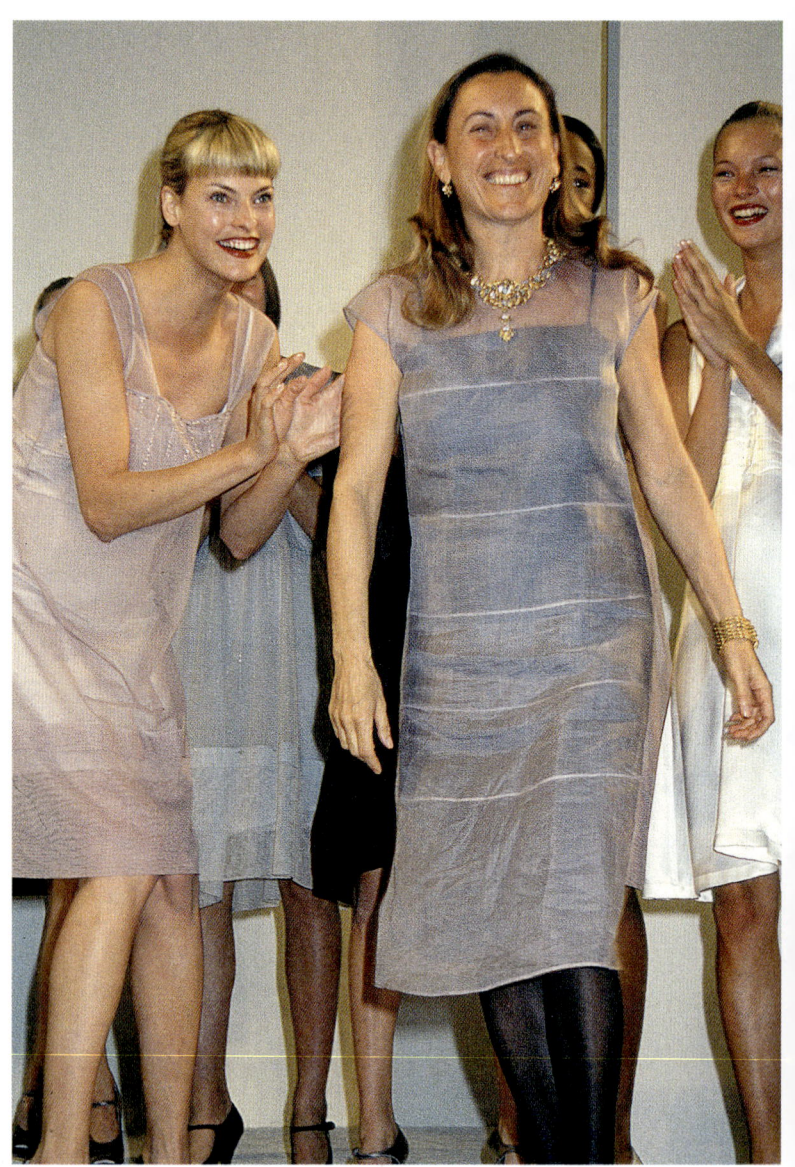

By 1994, Miu Miu made its runway debut. The Spring/Summer 1995 collection was shown in New York on October 30, 1994. Cementing the brand early on as one that marketed to very specific tastes and interrogated the concept of high fashion, the collection was full of silky, shiny fabrics and underwear as outerwear, a Miu Miu staple forever. Models wore their hair messy and tousled, with little slip dresses and sheer skirts revealing bright red underwear. Button-down shirts were left undone, deep scarlet red blazers were worn with nothing else underneath and the combinations of gossamer-fine fabrics with more utilitarian options created a visually striking and mentally intriguing dialogue. If it was sexy, it was sexy through the female gaze. The *Daily Mail* called out the collection for its "slew of see-through dresses worn over garish red underwear."

For three seasons, including the Spring/Summer 1995 collection, Miu Miu continued to show its runway collections in New York before taking the collections to London and then later, Milan and eventually, Paris. In these very early collections, Miuccia Prada continued to solidify Miu Miu as a brand that looked at womanhood from a unique perspective, interrogating all facets of being a woman and being perceived as one and what it means. This came courtesy of a designer who has often said, "I say to myself every single morning, 'I have to decide if I am a 15-year-old girl or a lady near death.'" In the world of Miu Miu, "dressing your age" doesn't exist. Just look at the Spring/Summer 1997 collection, presented in London. The inspiration was the story of "a very young girl working at the circus". Here, there were elements of style remixed, like schoolgirl pleated skirts and business casual collared shirts as well as pyjama-like tunics, hoodies and lingerie-light slips. The elements of done and undone – now intrinsic to Miu Miu – were all there.

OPPOSITE Miuccia Prada with supermodels Linda Evangelista and Kate Moss backstage after her debut Miu Miu show in 1994.

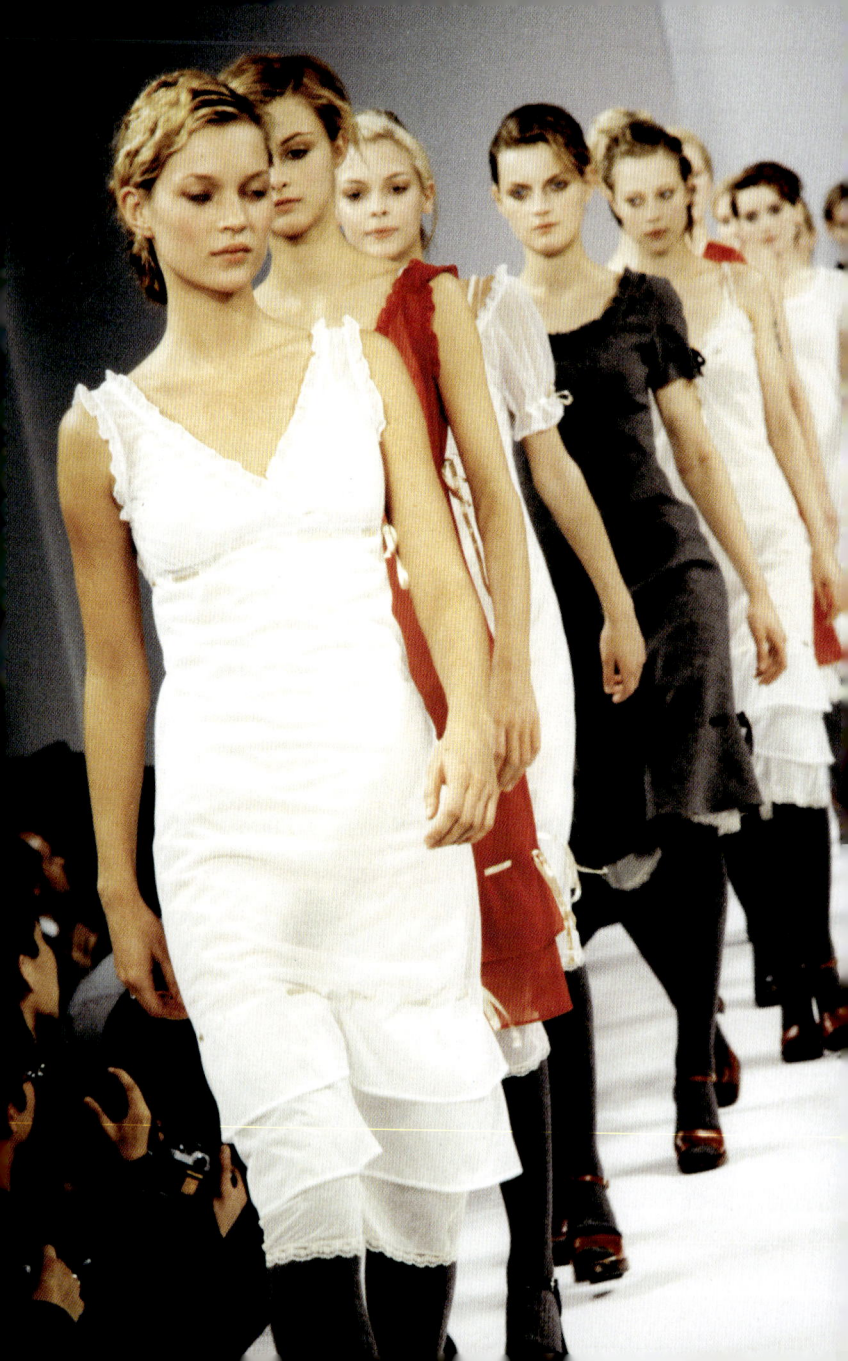

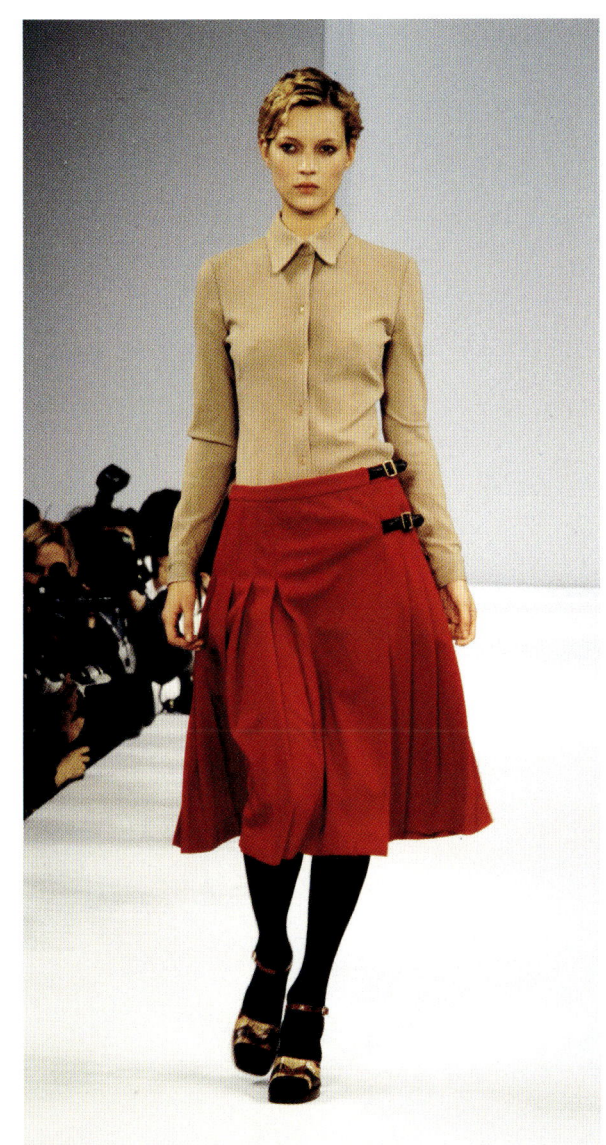

RIGHT For Autumn/
Winter 1996,
Kate Moss wore a
button-down top
and pleated skirt,
both inspired by the
uniform dressing
which Miuccia Prada
often references.

OPPOSITE Miu Miu
often plays with
icons of femininity –
like the slip dress or
the baby doll dress.

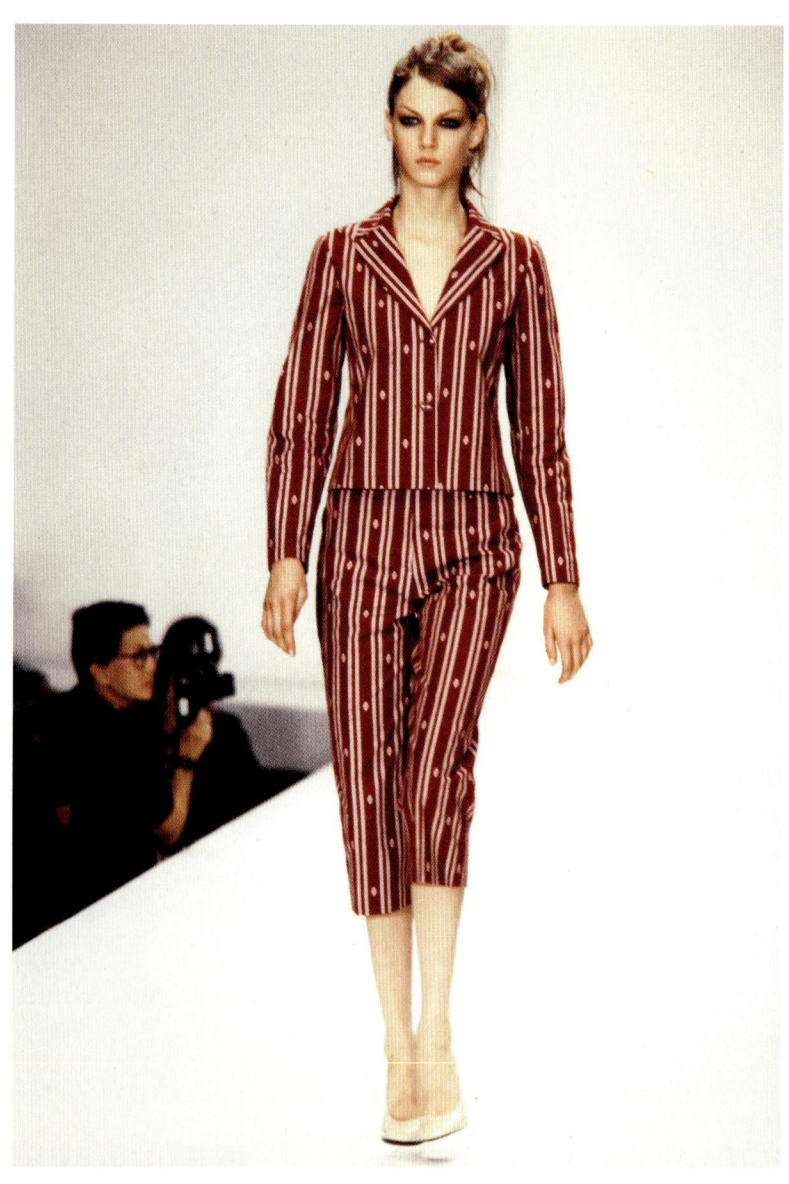

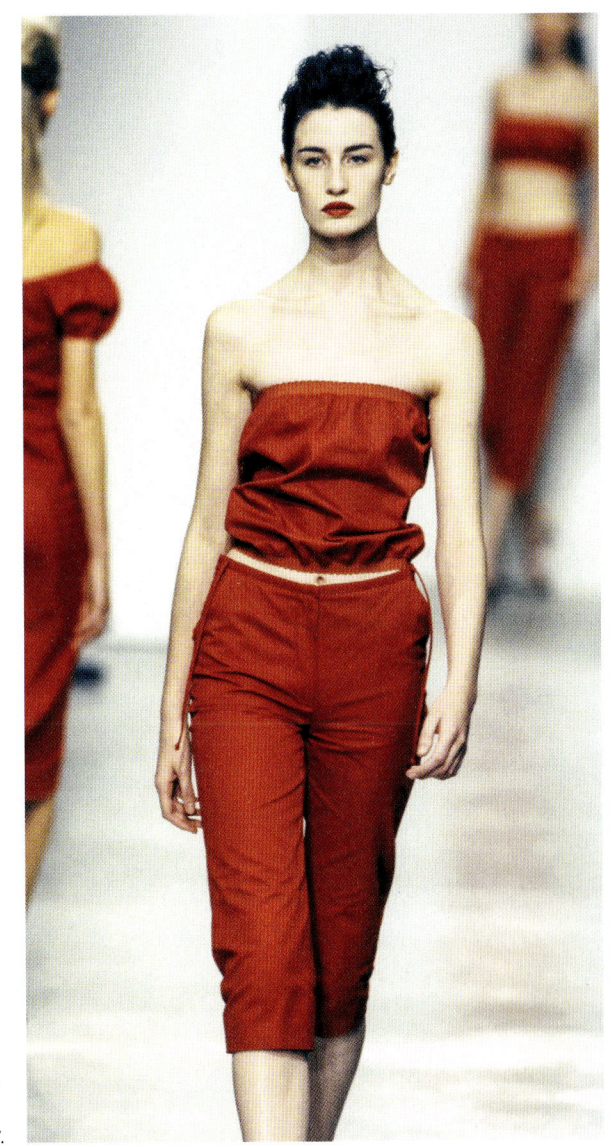

RIGHT Erin O'Connor models a simple yet dramatic look from Miu Miu Spring/ Summer 1998.

OPPOSITE Even if Miu Miu was cast as a minimal brand in its early days, it was easy to see Miuccia Prada's take on maximalist prints, as with this look from Spring/Summer 1997.

In the early days, Miu Miu didn't look like Prada, but it did bear some resemblance to the Prada brand. Just like a sister. Miuccia Prada was designing both Prada and Miu Miu in the earliest days, reportedly creating the Miu Miu collections in just 15 days, after completing Prada. "The more they told me that I should differentiate, the more I enjoyed doing in Prada what I should have done in Miu Miu, and vice versa," Miuccia told *W*. "I like to mix up my ideas." In 1981, Fabio Zambernardi joined the design team as a collaborator and eventually became the design director, working at Miu Miu

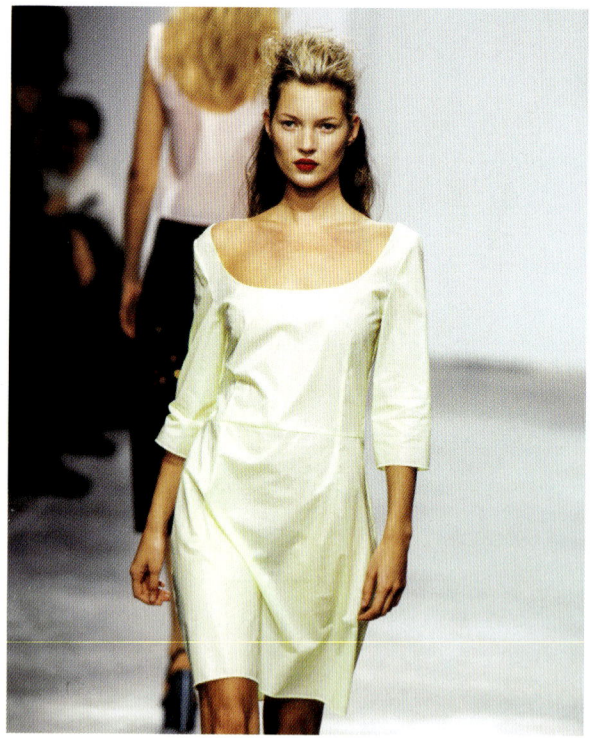

RIGHT The paper-thin dresses of Spring/Summer 1998 had Miu Miu's classic element of unexpected undoneness.

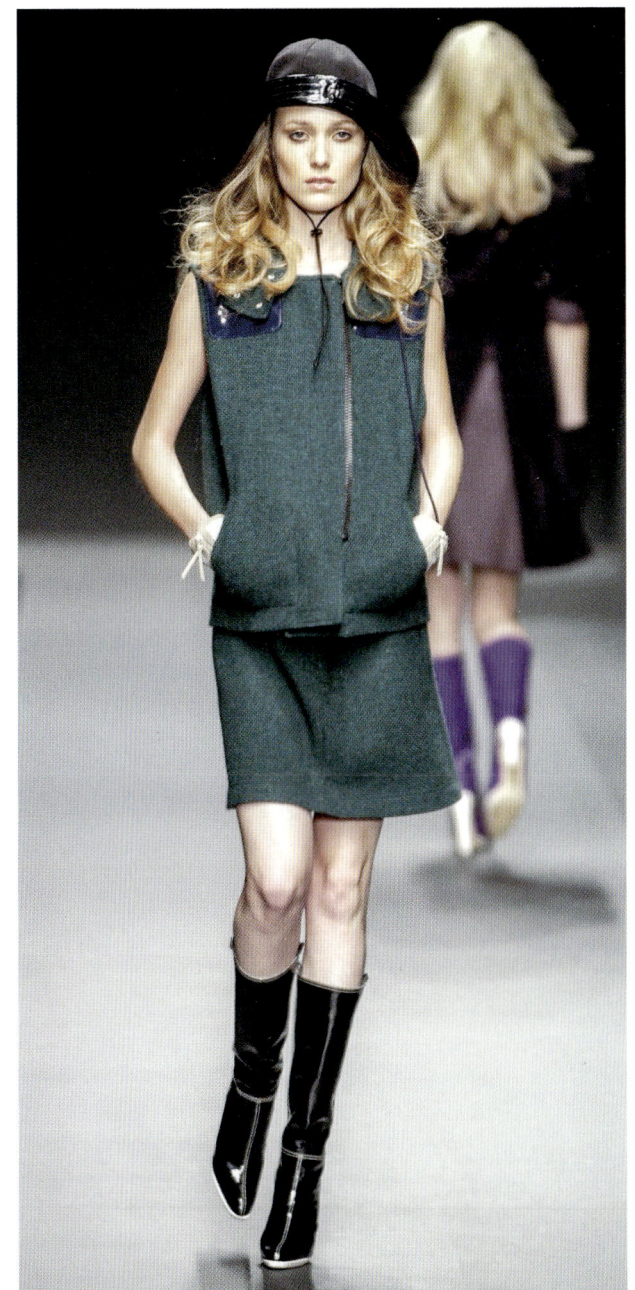

RIGHT The styling and the addition of a chic little hat, seen for Autumn/Winter 2002, are a key example of the brand experimenting with accessories.

and Prada until 2023. He would go on to gain notoriety in the industry for his contributions to the brands. He once told *Business of Fashion*, "To be contemporary, modern, I never know really what it means to be fashionable, a word that I find terrible and boring."

For Autumn/Winter 2001, even after being around for nearly a decade, Miu Miu was still experimenting with lingerie dressing. The designer created an assortment of sheer black dresses, wicked goth-chic capes, and pretty floral tops and dresses in shades of soft amber and lilac, so attuned to the vintage aesthetic of the 1970s. These dresses hugged the body and were cut sheer, styled without bras. The Autumn/ Winter 2003 collection saw a bit of a transition, showcasing furs, graphic black and white motifs on wool fabrics and tweeds. Sweaters were layered over tops and styled with sheer skirts. Collars popped under coats. Officewear slacks took a subversive turn with old-world furs and scrunched-up gloves.

It was 10 years from when Miu Miu was first founded, and in some ways, it was as if the brand made major progress towards growing up and transforming while still maintaining that signature look. Miuccia Prada was still pumping out irreverent collections touching on girlhood, womanhood and everything in between. For Spring/Summer 2004, the vibe shifted carefully towards bohemianism with a Miu Miu twist. Suede skirt suits and shirts with jewelled collars came together with floral patterned skirts and T-shirts featuring quirky graphics like ghosts. Punctuating the whole thing were the accessories, which would later become a Miu Miu signature. Belts were thrown over cardigans, blazers and tops (Miuccia herself wore one over her ombré cardigan as she took the final bow) and cascades of feathers topped the models' heads.

OPPOSITE For Autumn/Winter 2003, Miu Miu showed models in belted fur coats with gloves, but the proportions and styling represent the brand's affinity for quirkiness over conventional ladylike aesthetics.

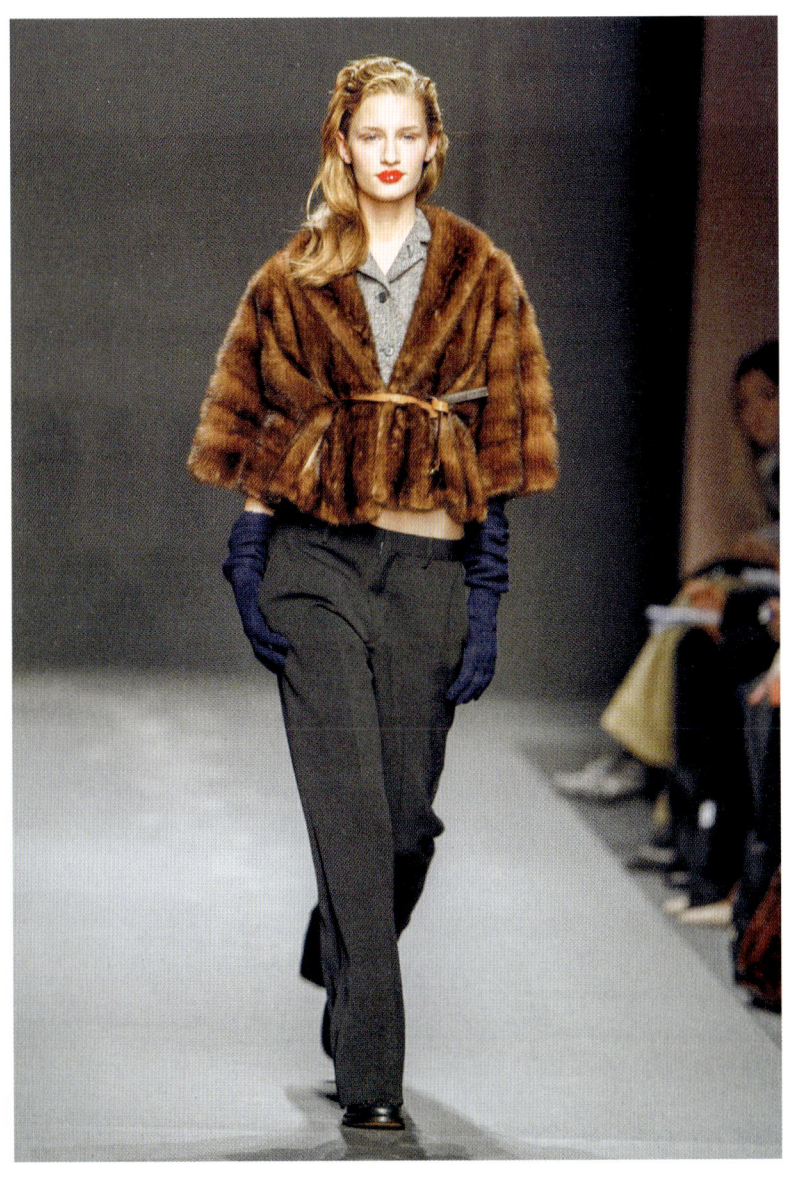

Androgyny at Miu Miu

Miuccia Prada turned her distinctive eye towards the world of menswear in 1998. The first version of Miu Miu menswear was presented for the Spring/Summer 1999 co-ed collection. It was highly androgynous. Both the male and female models wore minimalist, sporty looks that mixed that certain off-kilter energy Miu Miu became famous for. Think: things that wouldn't normally be paired together or colours that clashed beautifully. Crisp blazers were paired with hiking sandals and khaki shorts. Suits somehow looked shrunken and baggy at the same time. Utilitarian vests paired with wool shorts and deep cobalt suits resembled boiler suits. Miu Miu menswear could easily have been shared between all the Miu Miu women on the runway. At least, the long, lean, unisex silhouettes proved that. At the time, Stefano Pilati, who would later go on to be the creative director for Yves Saint Laurent, worked on the design team at Miu Miu.

For Autumn/Winter 1999, Miu Miu presented its second debut of menswear, once again shown as a co-ed collection. With an apocalyptic, neutral-hued palette, the models wore skinny, tailored pieces with a sporty edge. There were plenty of cropped pants, little leather bomber jackets, workwear-inspired dresses with hoods, and for men, sleeveless hooded jackets with trousers and clunky boots, and perfectly baggy suits. As per usual, the aesthetic was such that the clothes could have been swapped on any gender and still looked perfectly at home. "I think young guys are so charming," Miuccia Prada told the *New York Times* of the collection, "I like the way young people are different and so sweet with each other."

Tapping into menswear, Miuccia Prada's work for Miu Miu seemed to lean slightly more minimal. At the time, Miu Miu was also priced more affordably than Prada and introducing menswear was a way to expand the business. "The Four Horsemen of the

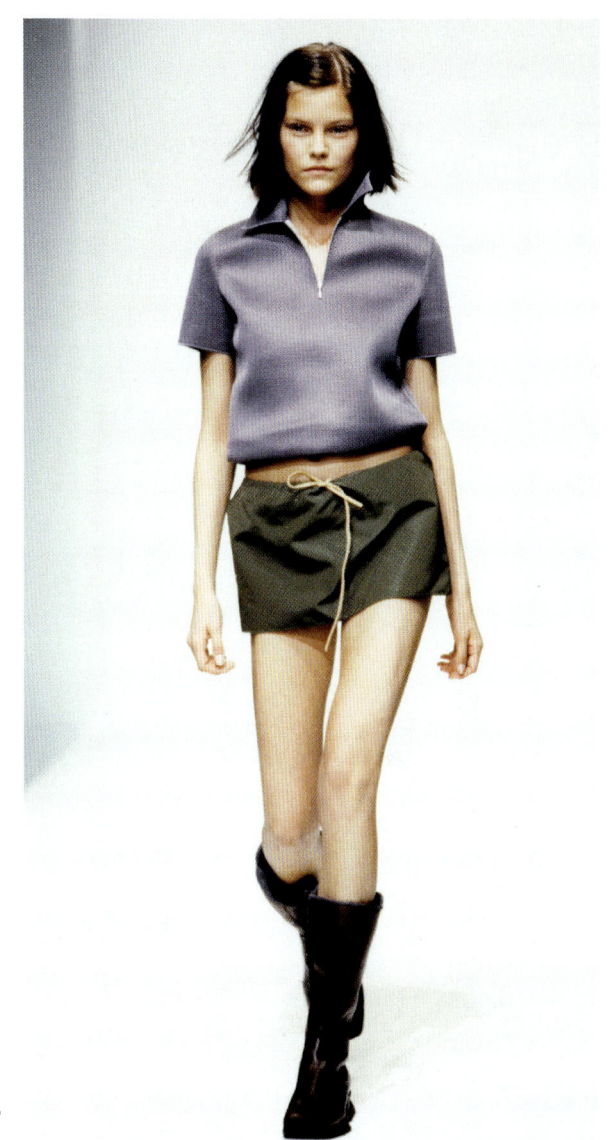

RIGHT Miu Miu's minimalist, sporty side could be seen in the Spring/Summer 1999 collection.

OVERLEAF There was nothing else like Miu Miu menswear. The brand played with conventional gender aesthetics and often leaned into minimalism.

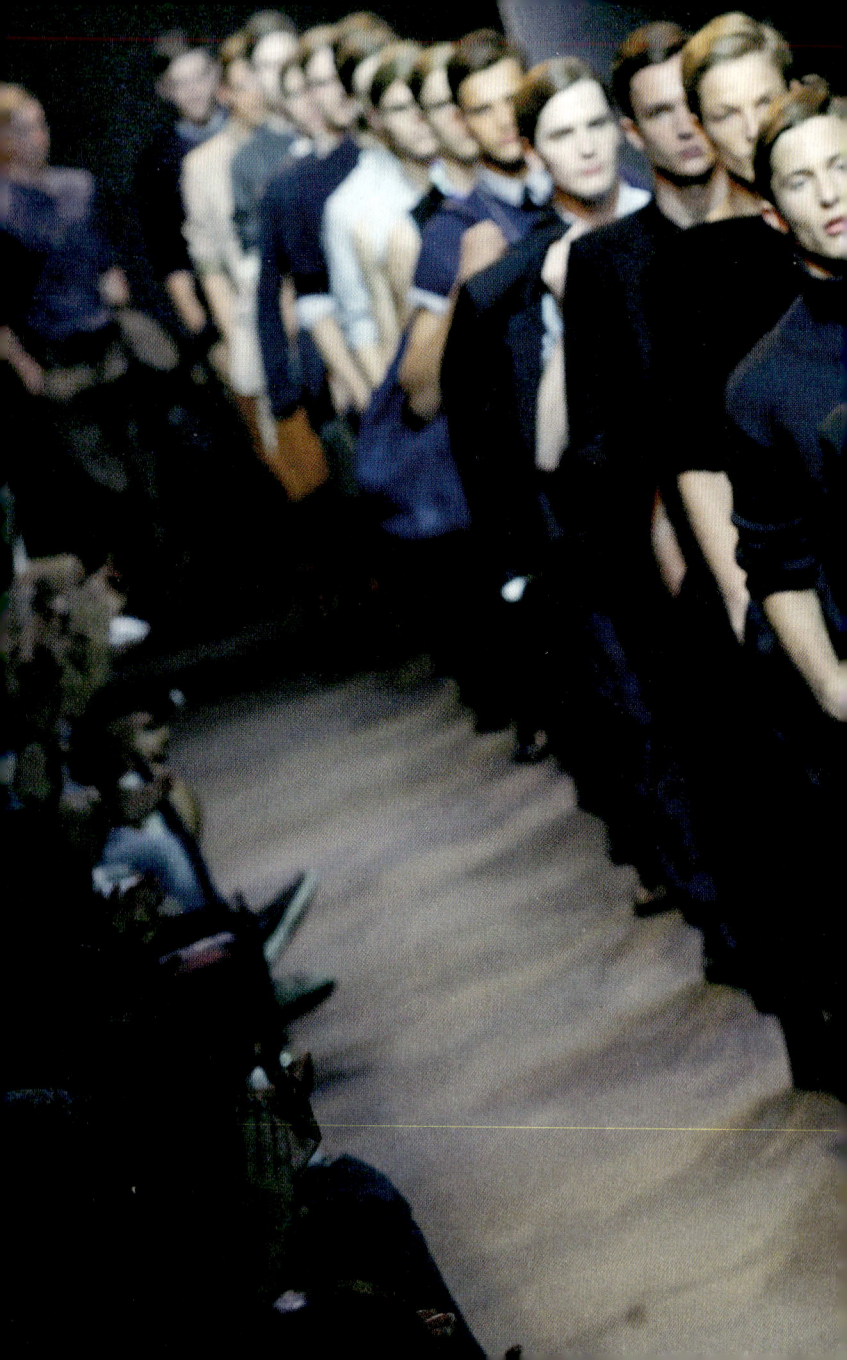

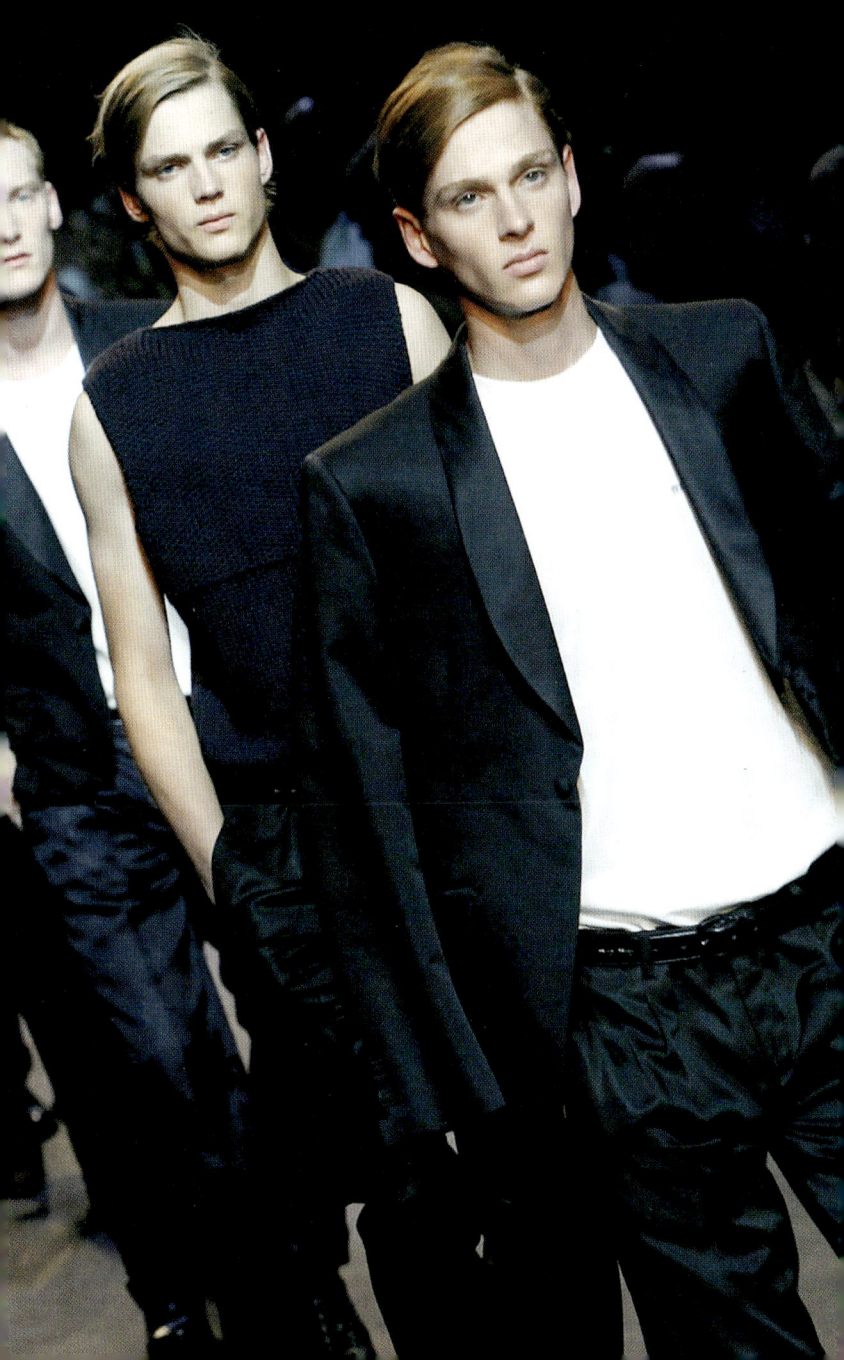

Minimal-ypse – Miuccia Prada, Jil Sander, Calvin Klein and Mr. Lang, who rode black, white, gray and khaki horses, respectively – thundered on, bent on worldwide expansion," wrote the *New York Times* in 1998. Miu Miu menswear would continue for one decade before it was discontinued in 2008, but it would never be forgotten by its diehard fans. After all, the aesthetic was irreplaceable, even all these years later. "There was an unorthodox feminine thread running through the styling, which was most obvious in the way everything – from a purple duffle coat to a stolid tweed suit – was belted," fashion critic Tim Blanks wrote of a collection in 2005. *WWD* reported that the decision to shut down the menswear label was made because Miu Miu's parent company wanted to shift focus to the women's side of the label.

In 2006, Miu Miu moved its shows to Paris Fashion Week and claimed its spot on the last day of the fashion week, and therefore the finale of fashion month. Prada chief executive officer Patrizio Bertelli told *WWD*, "Miu Miu is a brand with its own identity. It has grown considerably in terms of content and quality. We want our clients and the industry to clearly understand this." In 2005, Miu Miu had nearly 30 stores globally and posted sales of €129 million, or $161.25 million.

With the move to Paris, Miu Miu took on a more maximalist direction, diving headfirst into quirky femininity through excess and opulence. Explosions of colours and patterns, plus over-the-top accessories, were the name of the game. Socks, gloves, hats, necklaces, earrings, rings – everything. If the Miu Miu of the past was more concerned with a subversive ladylike and meek aesthetic, the Miu Miu of the mid 2000s was big on personality. The look was best seen in 2006, where star-printed slip dresses were styled over white T-shirts, with matching opera gloves, sky-high heels, blackout sunglasses and beehive hairdos.

OPPOSITE For Spring/Summer 2005, Miu Miu proved that the brand has an incredible and unique perspective on prints.

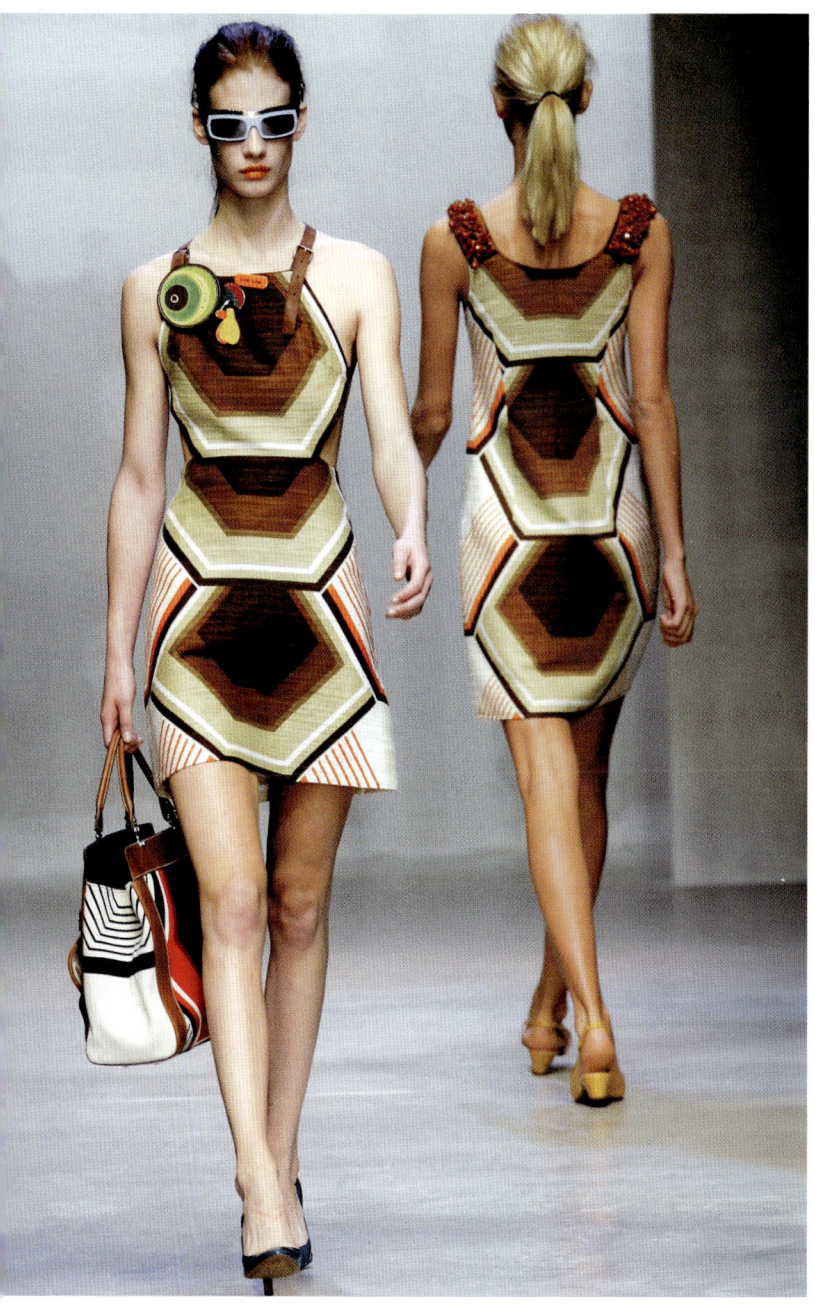

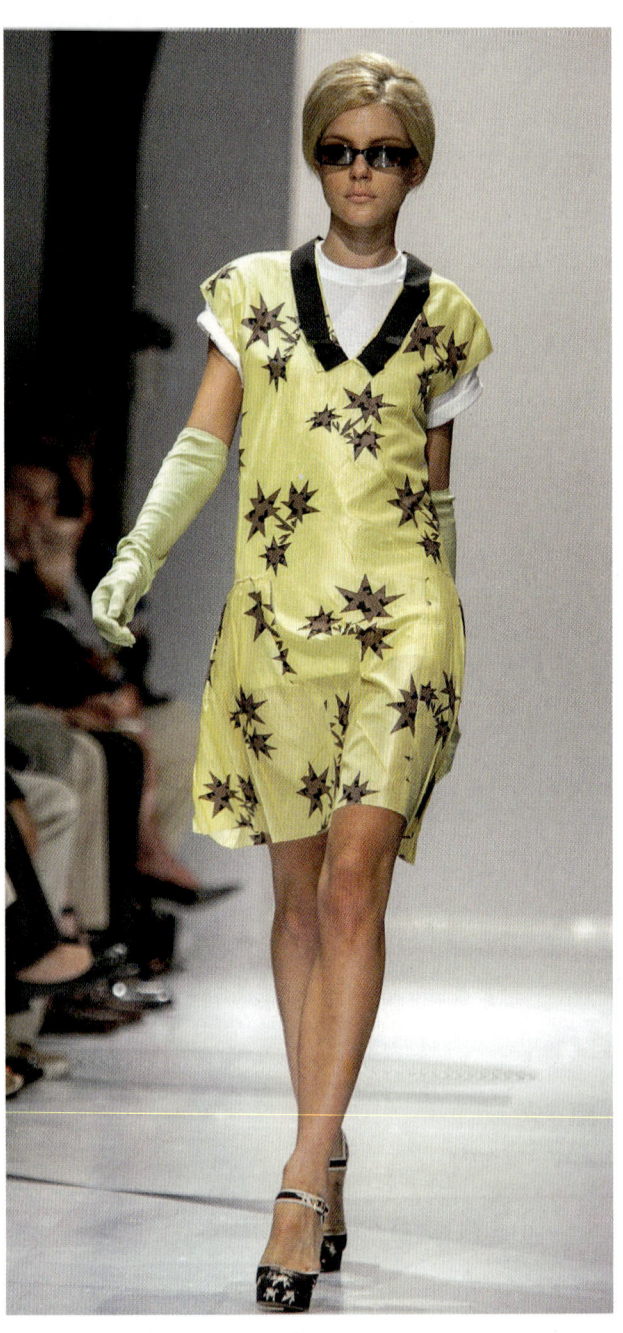

LEFT The Spring/ Summer 2006 show was one of its most maximalist yet, from the prints to the accessories and even the beehive hair.

OPPOSITE For Autumn/Winter 2006, it seemed like the brand really hit its stride – melding old and new elements of feminine tropes with layers of interesting quirks for maximal impact.

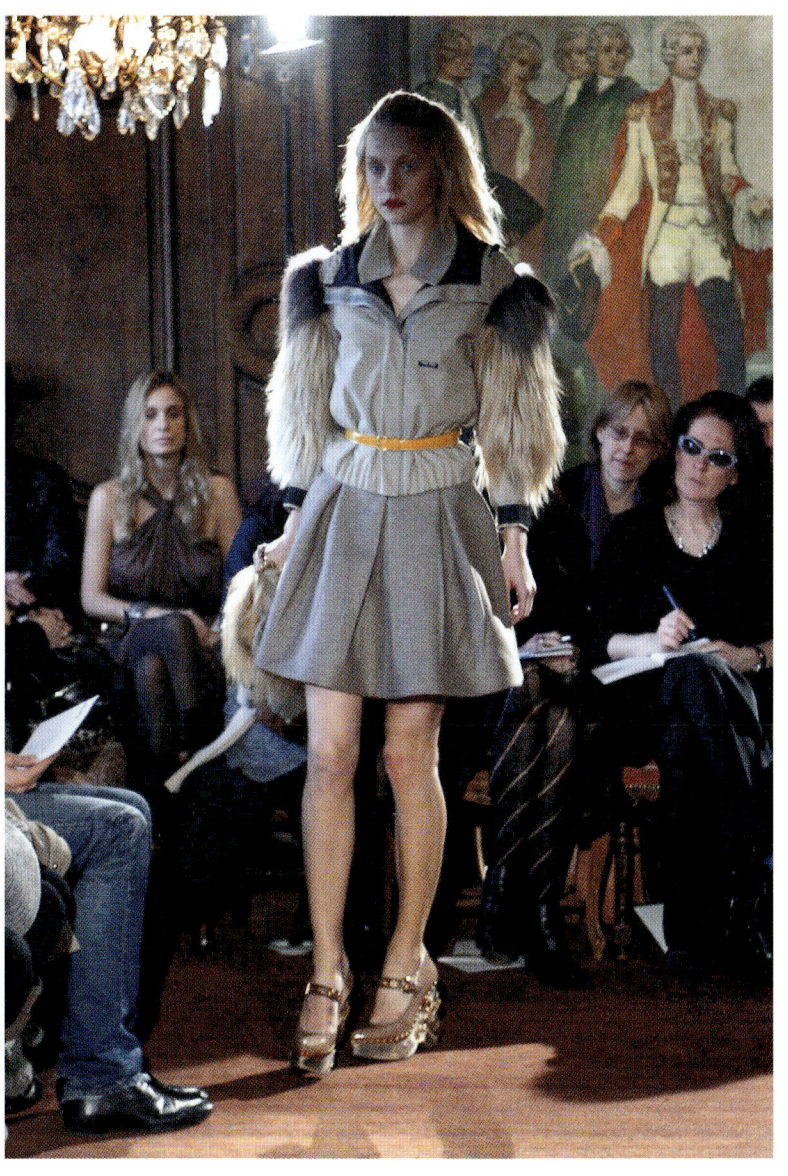

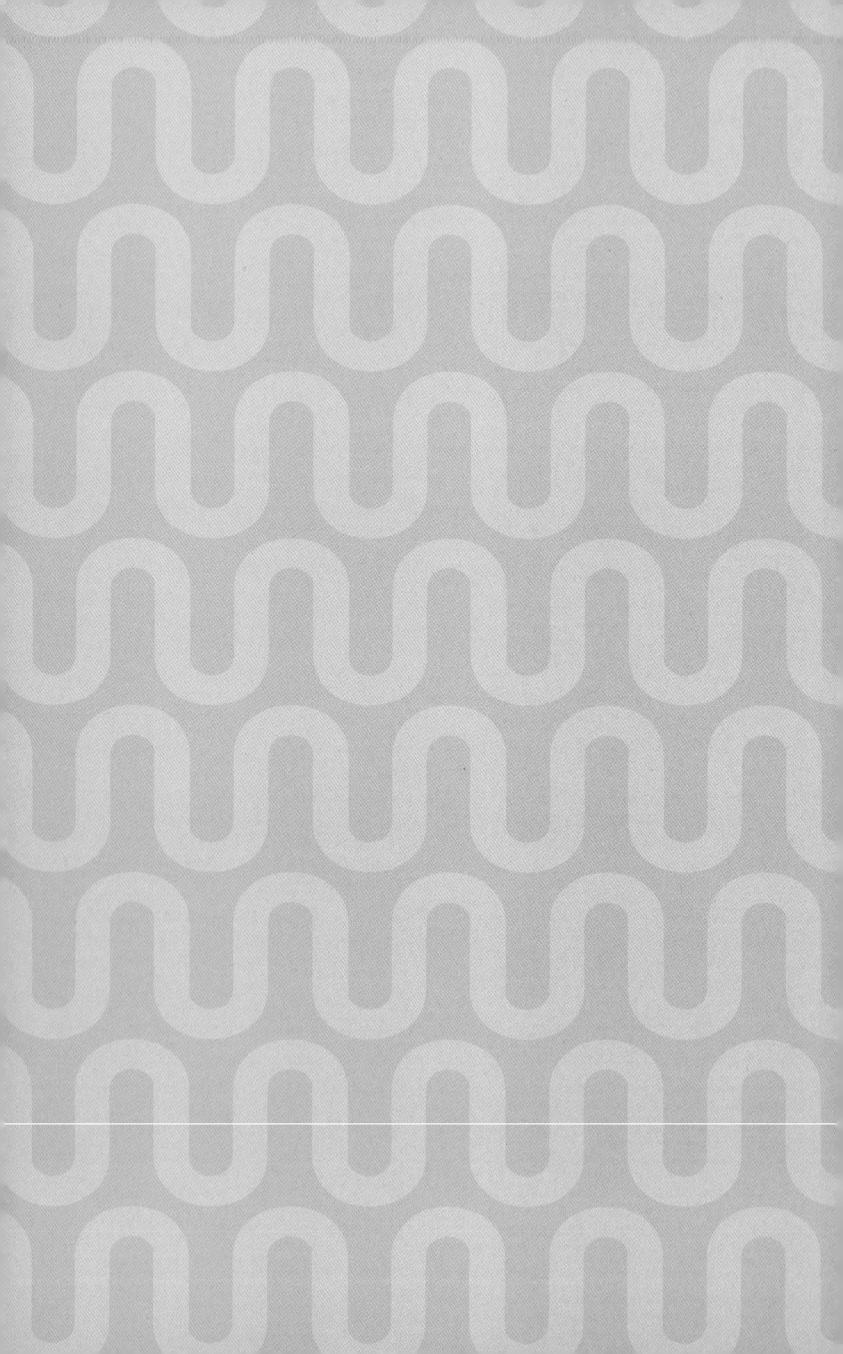

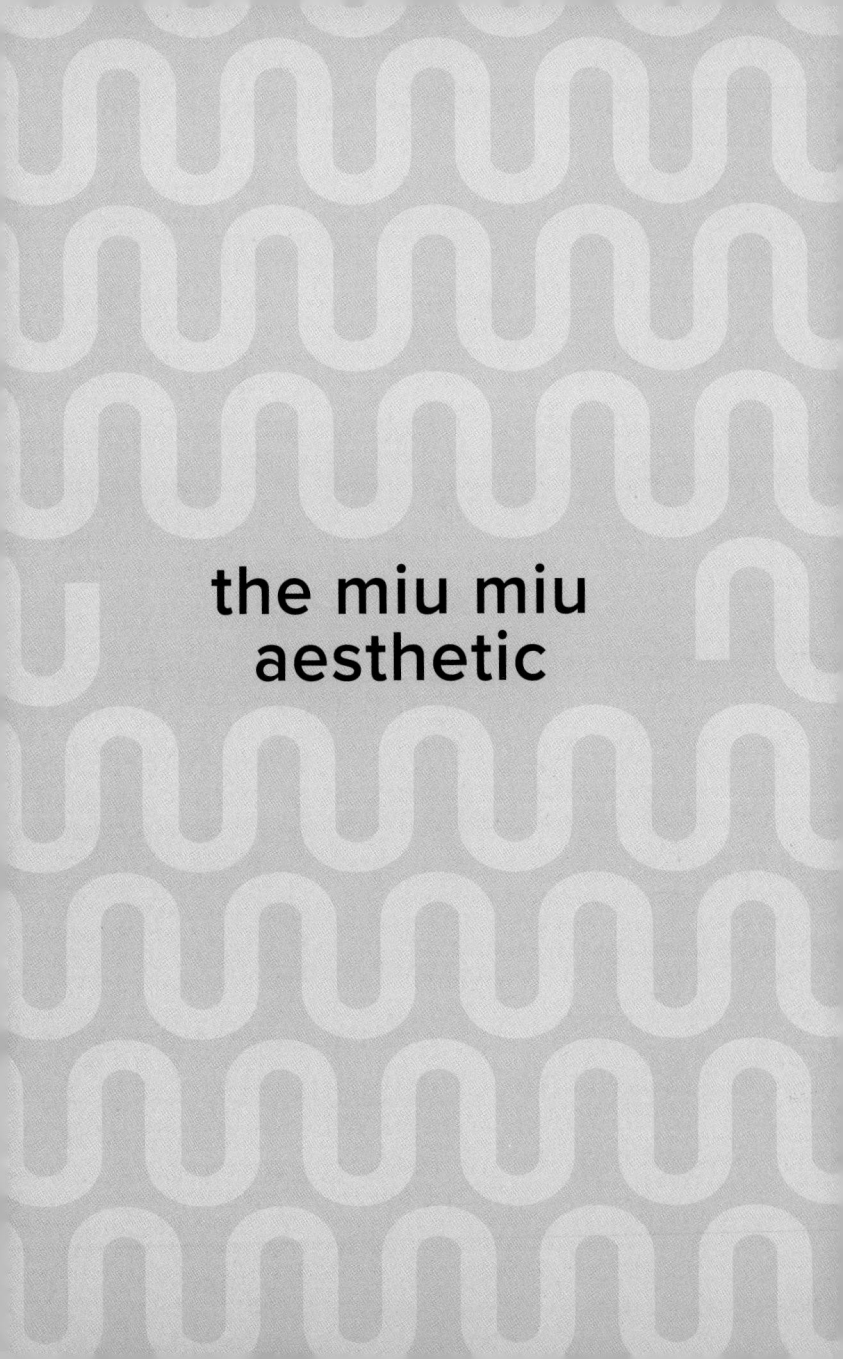

the miu miu
aesthetic

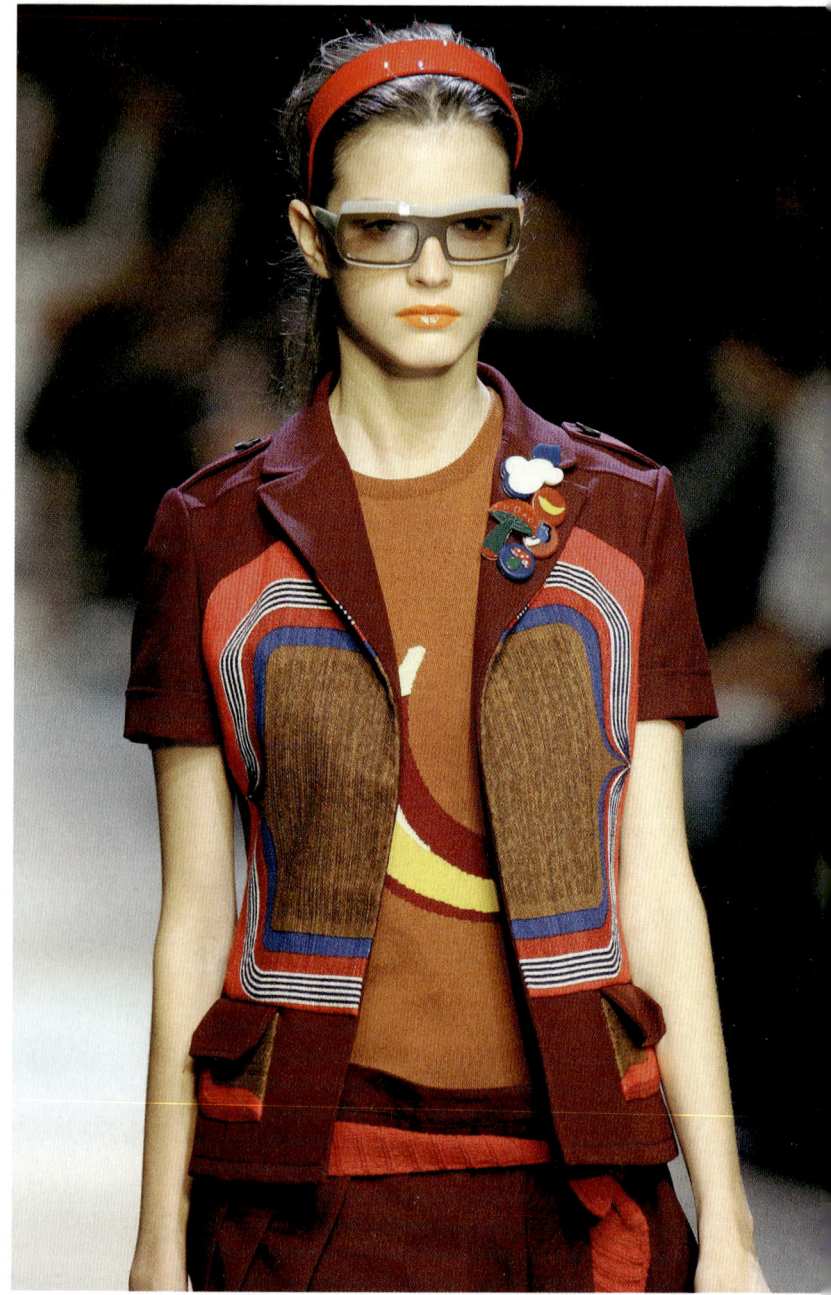

the magic of
miu miu

Miu Miu has lived several lives when it comes to aesthetics. It's gone from boho to minimal to maximalist and back again in several different ways. There is no single aesthetic for Miu Miu because it's a prism of expression for Miuccia Prada and her moods. "I get bored very quickly. That is why I like fashion," she told *Harper's Bazaar*.

From the very first collection, Miu Miu played with elements of boho, Western style and girlishness with a studied dose of utilitarian minimalism. Like many brands of the mid to late 1990s, understated minimalism reigned supreme, but Miu Miu always had its own quirks. Take, for example, the Autumn/Winter 1998 show which juxtaposed Miuccia Prada's own idea of what retro-futuristic, space-age design looks like, along with all the classic Miu Miu-isms. Starting in 2006, when Miu Miu made its Paris Fashion Week debut, the brand introduced a new kind of intrepid feminine maximalism, experimenting with that look until around 2018. From thereon out, Miu Miu has played with all sides of the brand, hitting on the house codes shown since day one.

The phrase *ugly chic* has often been used to describe the work of Miuccia Prada, and it holds completely true for Miu Miu. Even at its most sexy, with skin bared or hemlines cut high, the fashion itself is like a mirror reflecting and refracting

OPPOSITE The retro colours and prints of Spring/Summer 2005 best represent the brand's perspective: unique and unafraid to be different.

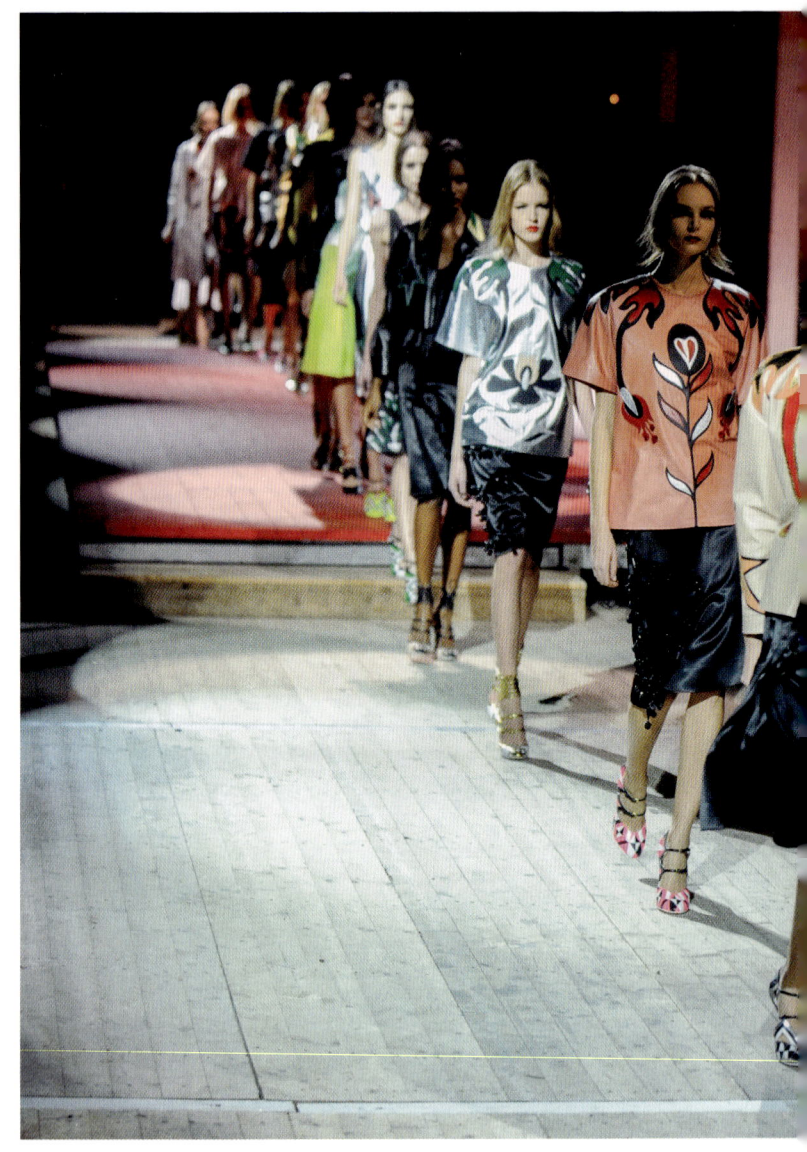

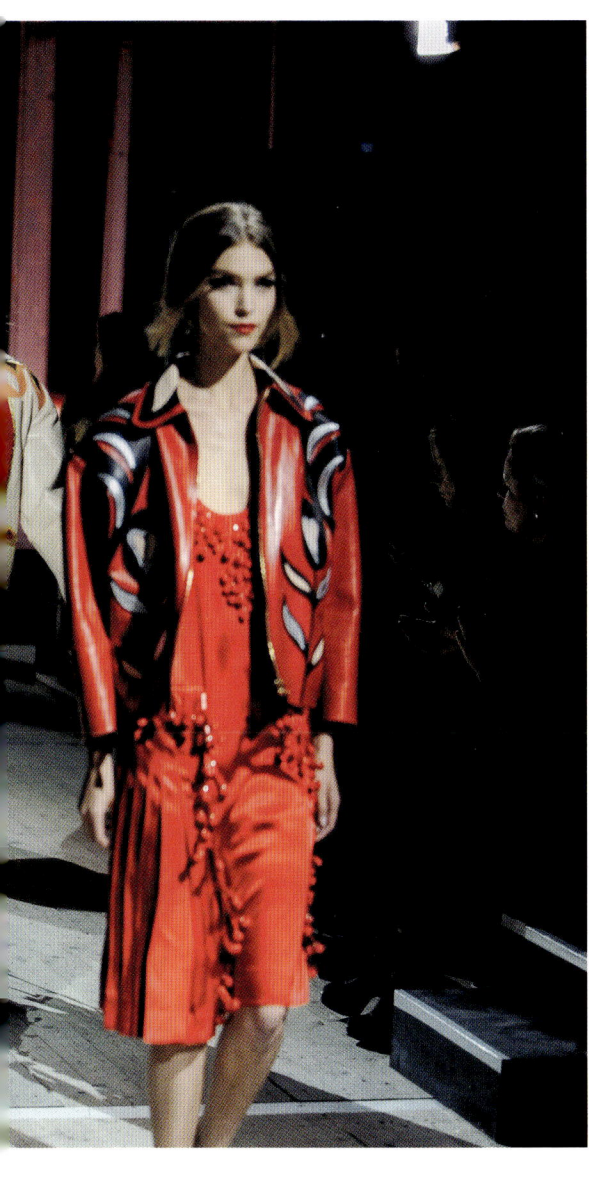

LEFT The artful
leather jackets from
Spring/Summer 2011
are a favourite of Miu
Miu maximalists.

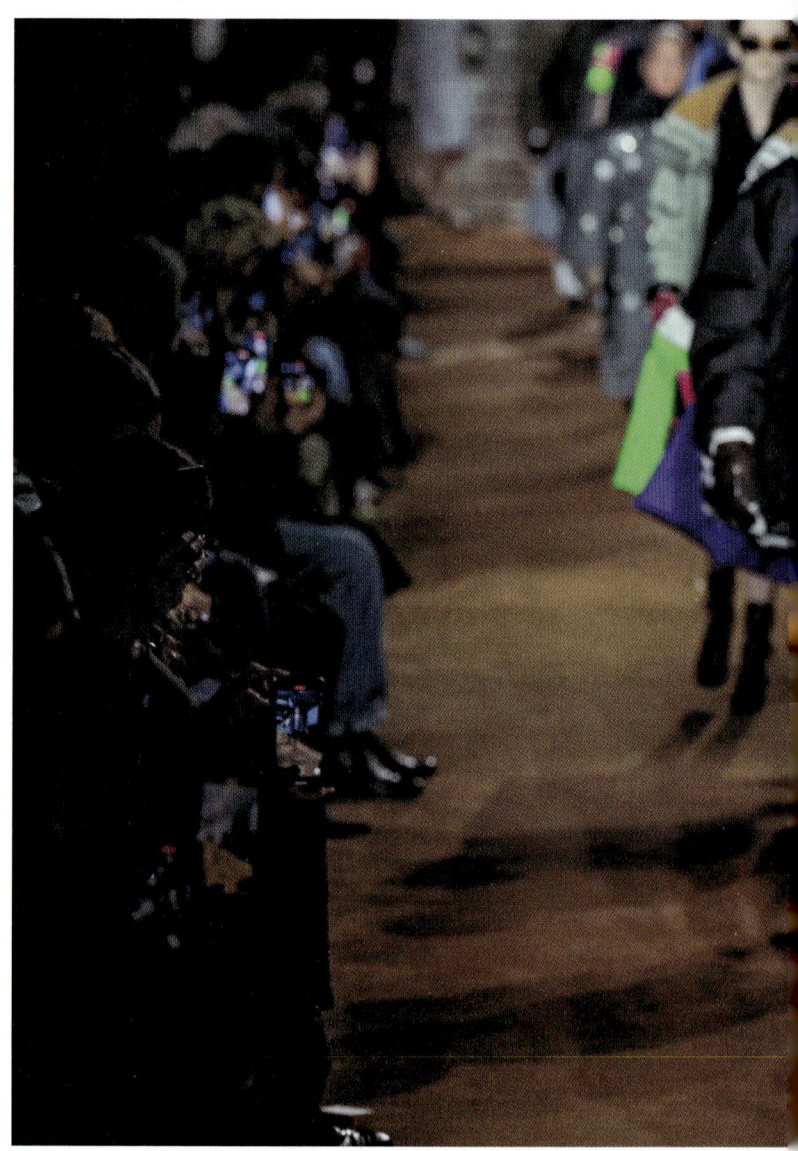

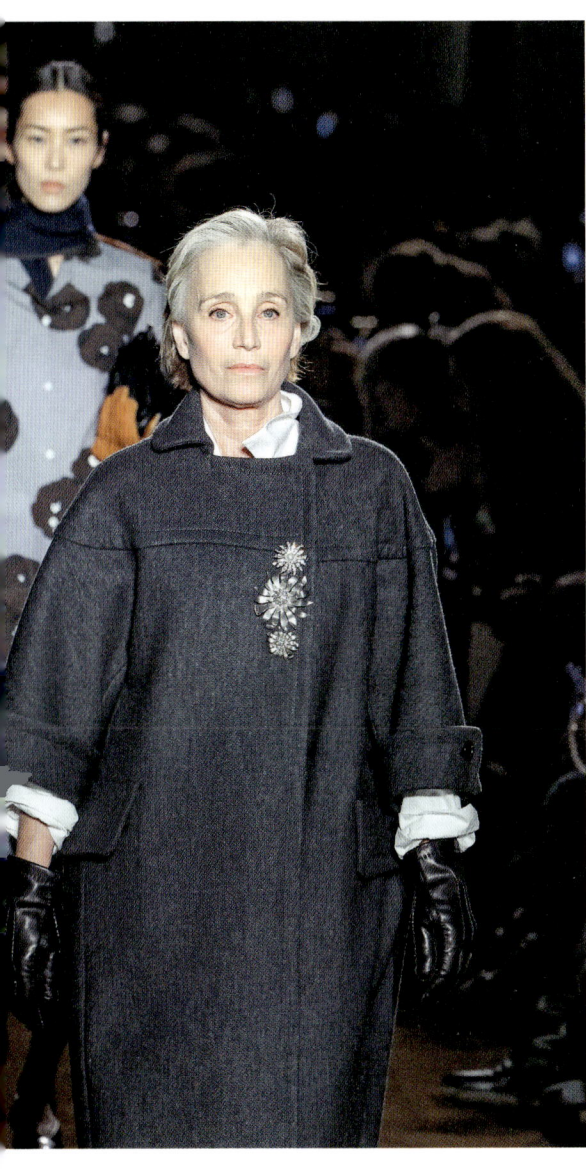

LEFT Off-kilter
colours, signature
prints and unusual
shapes from the
Autumn/Winter 2024
collection.

the world of Miuccia Prada. It's designed for the female gaze. "Probably what I want in my life to attack most is the idea of beauty and sexiness. That is my obsession," she told *W* magazine. Especially in the early days and mid 2010s, Miu Miu felt inherently individualistic. Perceivably "ugly" to some because they might not understand the intrinsic language nor the high fashion interpretations created by Miuccia Prada. Underwear as outerwear that's not instantly sexy? Skintight plaid onesies? A dress covered in cat prints and bedecked in chunky crystals? All part of the Miu Miu universe at one point in time. "Ugly is attractive, ugly is exciting. Maybe because it is newer," she told *Document Journal*.

Taste, in the world of Miu Miu, is also subjective. "Miu Miu is all about bad taste," Miuccia Prada told *Vogue* in 1995. "For me it's either total elegance or total bad taste. We call Miu Miu the bad girls. It's innocent young girls pretending to be elegant and not making it. Not having a concept of what is right, to me that is very sexy."

Critically, Miu Miu is undoubtedly one of the most interesting brands to think about in terms of aesthetics. "Prada's designs stem from an inner vision of herself," said the *New York Times* fashion critic Cathy Horyn in 2012, "and plainly it's filled with images from Italian films and conflicts involving beauty. But the upshot is a tangled, what-a-woman sexiness."

Above all else, Miuccia Prada presents as an intellectual designer, whether it's because of how the world of marketing has presented her or not. Perhaps one thing that undoubtedly contributes to Miu Miu's aesthetic, however, is the fact that she doesn't have the traditional training of a designer. She has no formal design training, doesn't sketch, and instead begins her designs with ideas.

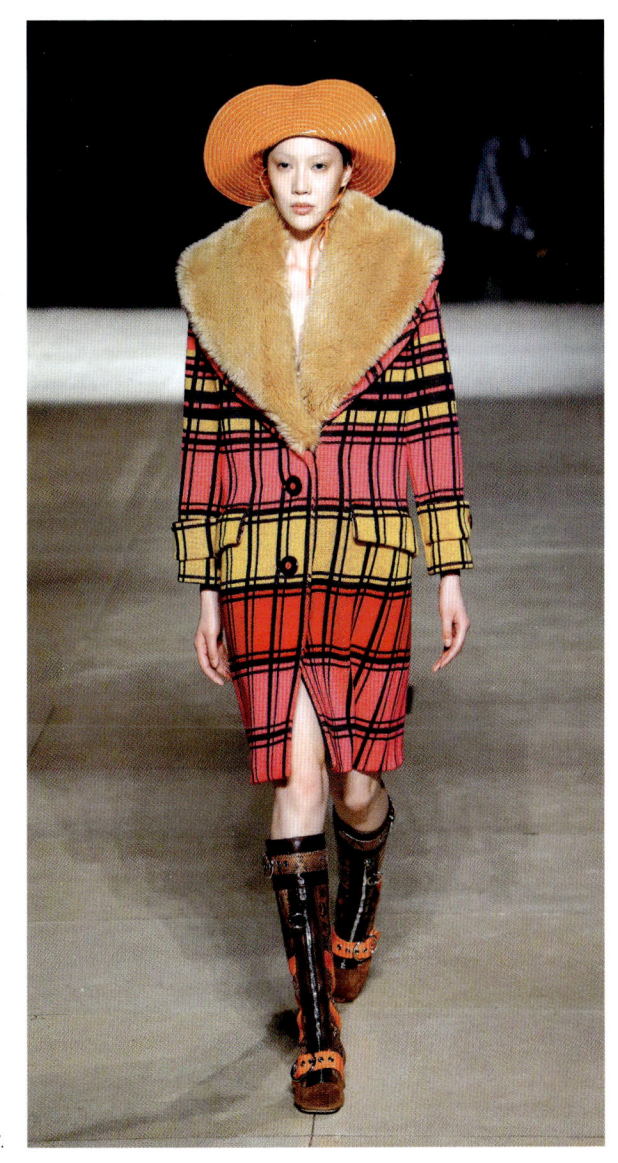

RIGHT Miu Miu went all out with print, colour, texture and accessories for Autumn/Winter 2017.

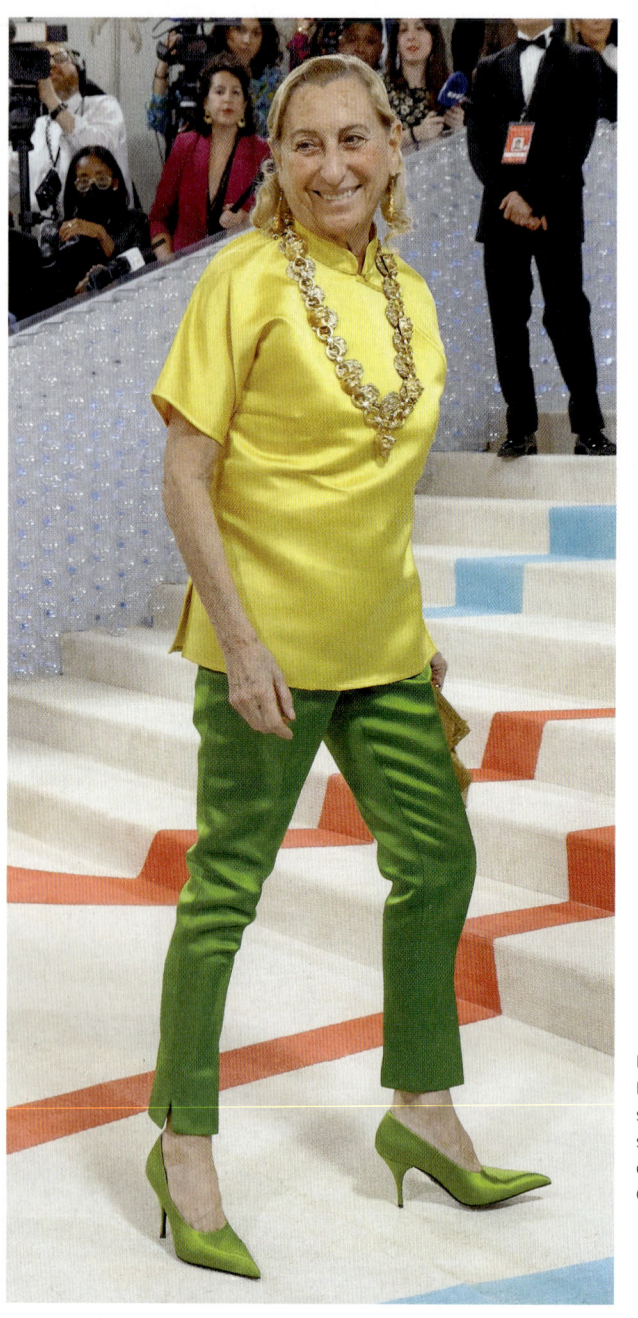

LEFT Miuccia
Prada has her own
signature style, as
seen here on the red
carpet for the Met
Gala.

Dressing Like Miuccia Herself

Miu Miu feels personal and unique, connected to how Miuccia Prada dresses in her own life. After all, this is a woman who could be described in some ways as an eccentric. Take, for example, the fact that she has a slide, designed by the German artist Carsten Höller, which goes from the inside of her personal office to the outside ground floor. Made of stainless steel, it has been installed in her Milan office since 2000.

When she comes out to take her bow at both Prada and Miu Miu shows, the audience is often as impressed and intrigued by her work on the runway as they are by her own personal sense of style. Always wearing her own work, she alternates between knee-length printed skirts, button-downs, simple wool sweaters, statement coats, satin suits and, often, mesmerizing jewellery. She could easily be crowned one of the most stylish designers of all time.

She's worn some of her best looks at the Met Gala, choosing a silky lemon-yellow top and lime green pants and matching pumps with a huge gold necklace in 2023. Likewise, she lit up the red carpet when she wore a highlighter green, plastic fringed dress to the 2018 "Heavenly Bodies: Fashion and the Catholic Imagination" Met Gala. The look was pulled directly from Prada's Autumn/Winter 2018 collection.

In the world of creative directors, it's typical to see some of the world's top designers wearing all black, or very simplified outfits. But that's never been the case for the iconoclastic Miuccia Prada, and as a result she stands out even more. At one point in time, her personal wardrobe was supplied by the Ferrari sisters, high-end tailors for children. According to a *New Yorker* article from 1994, "she had dresses and coats made to order, scaled up to her size and with 'corrections,' such as a bigger or smaller collar than the one that was there." It's no wonder, then, that Miu Miu takes girlish details

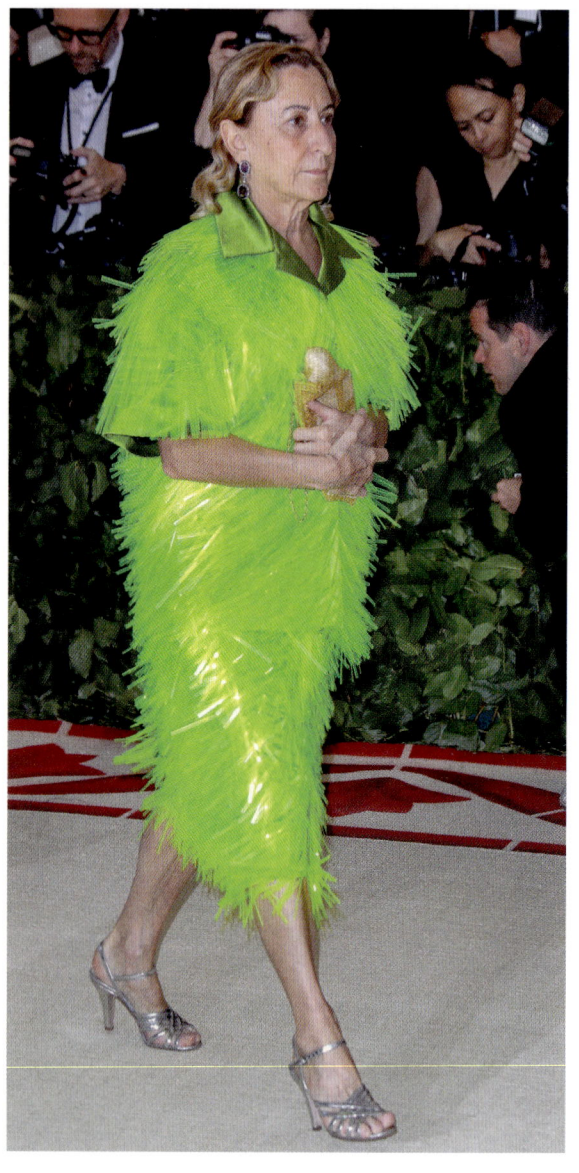

LEFT One of Miuccia Prada's iconic Met Gala red carpet looks: a piece plucked straight from the Prada runway.

OPPOSITE Miuccia Prada can often be seen wearing elements of uniforms, like pleated skirts.

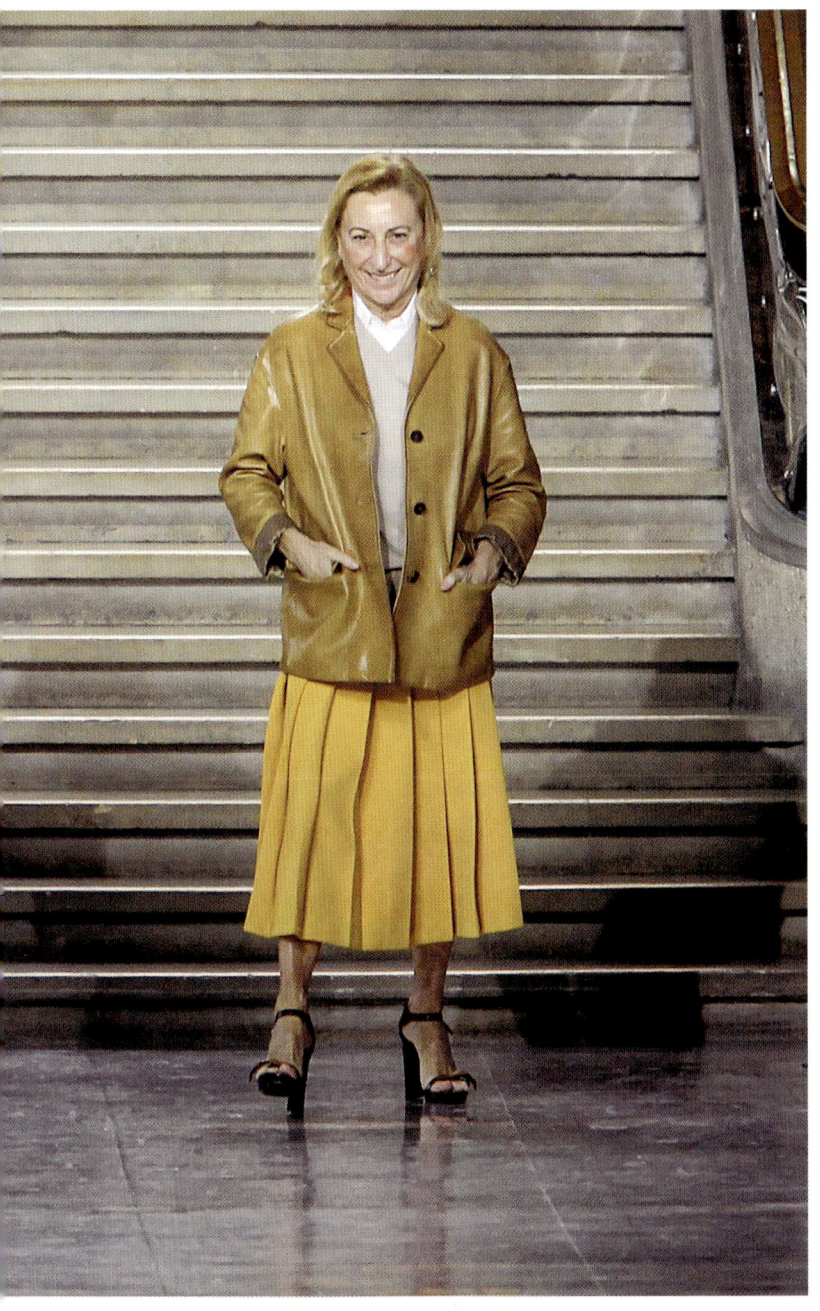

like ruffles, eyelets or little pleated miniskirts and throws them into the mix. The designs have often taken direct inspiration from little girls' clothes and blown them up into adult proportions, such as the dainty yet sculptural coats of the Spring/Summer 2016 collection. Miuccia Prada has also recalled that she started dressing up for school when she was 13 or 14, wearing gloves and knee-high socks – both elements that can also be seen in her collections.

Underwear as Outerwear

It may be mainstream now, but the concept of underwear as outerwear has been ingrained in Miu Miu since its very beginnings. It's almost impossible not to see different variations of it on the runway from the early '90s up until today. Take, for example, the Spring/Summer 1995 collection or the Spring/Summer 2023 collection. And yet, the brand has somehow radicalized the idea and reclaimed the concept to feel like it's cool in a non-sexy way. These are not clothes designed with the male gaze in mind. "The whole point of my job is trying to understand how women can be powerful but also feminine, and be believed and stay respected when everyone assumes those things mean you don't care about clothes," the designer once said of her Prada Autumn/Winter 2018 collection.

The Spring/Summer 2024 collection elevated American mall culture of the 2010s to a new level with layered polo shirts, knee-length baggy board shorts and leather bags stuffed to the brim with everything under the sun, including shoes. Also in the outfits? Miu Miu logo underwear peeking out from leather skirts and little ruffled puff miniskirts. At the show in Paris, many of the front-row guests wore the little hot pants and micro miniskirts from the previous season, proving dedication to the extreme look in real life.

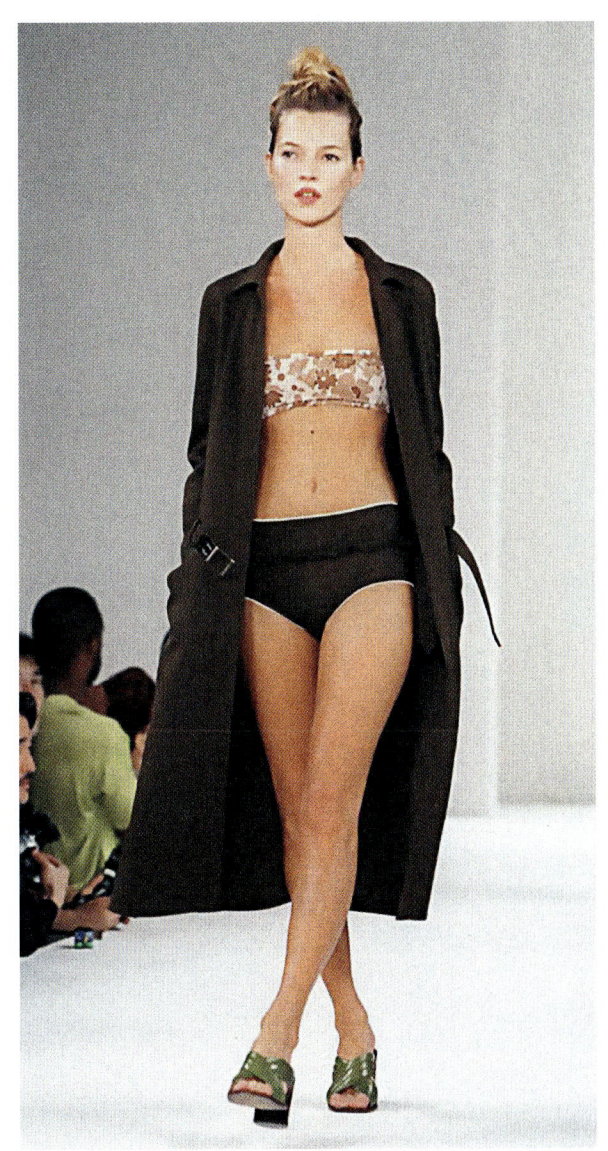

RIGHT The Miu Miu micro miniskirt went viral in 2022, but the brand has always experimented with super-short miniskirts and hot pants, as seen here on Kate Moss for Spring/Summer 1996.

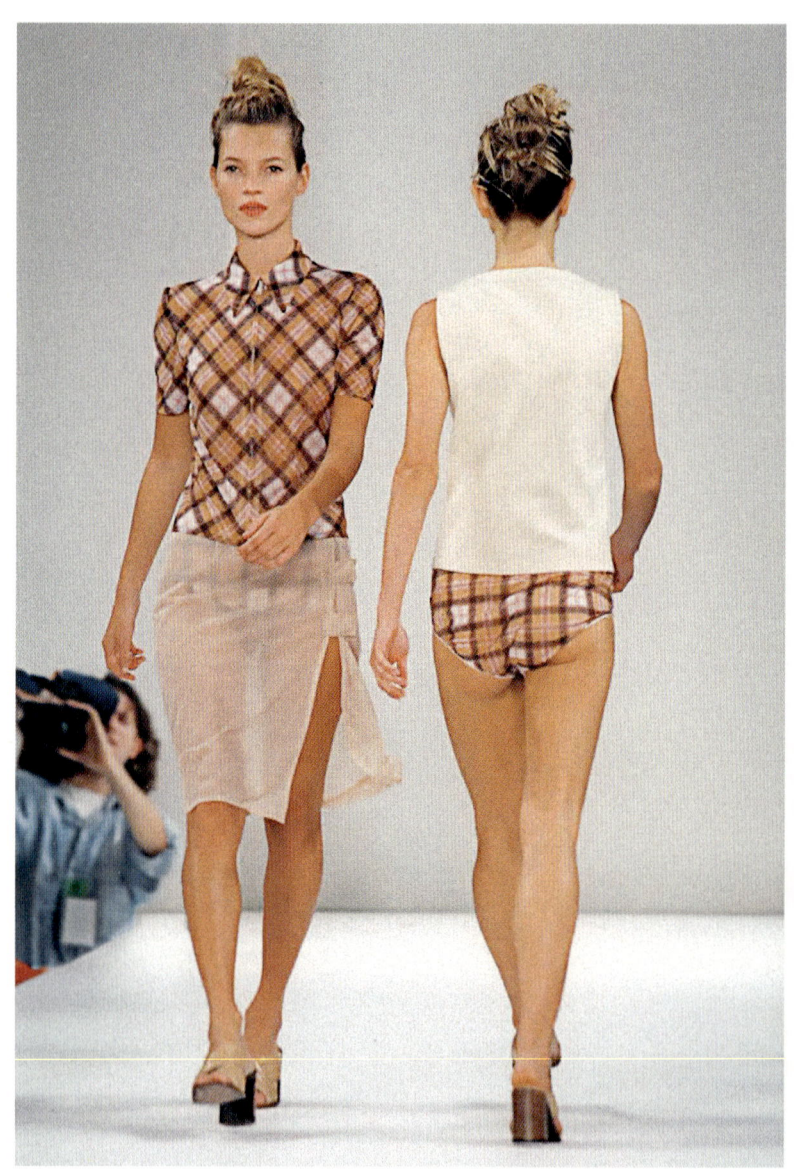

The Female Experience

Miu Miu plays with all aspects and aesthetics of womanhood. For Autumn/Winter 2024, there were big sweeping skirts paired with pearl necklaces and childlike, oversized mittens. Backstage, after the show, the designer said, "The point for me was really that you can choose different moments of your life. I have mixed them up."

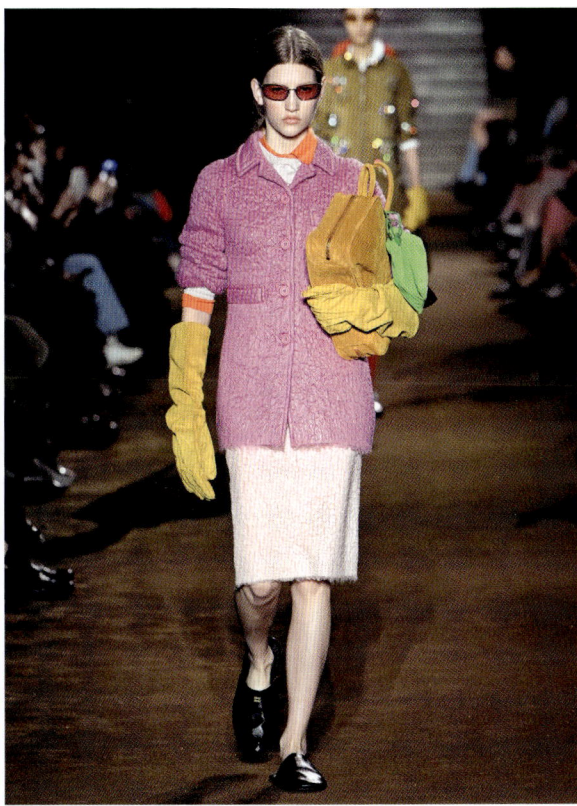

LEFT A look from Autumn/Winter 2024, emphasizing quirk and the worlds between girl and womanhood.

OPPOSITE Sheer skirts with visible underwear are a part of the Miu Miu playbook, as seen here on the Spring/Summer 1996 runway.

Throughout almost every single Miu Miu collection, it's possible to see some code of traditional female aesthetic – both projected and perceived. For example, the apron, a symbol once so tied to women's inescapable role as homemakers throughout history. For the Spring/Summer 2009 season, Miu Miu showed aprons transformed into chic little coverings over pleated dresses. They were thrown off to the side on printed skirts, or draped across the front of a minidress. "Why aprons? Why a symbol of women tied to the kitchen? Why now – when the return of the power woman has been a constant theme of the summer 2009 season? 'I like them,' Miuccia Prada said disingenuously of the mini pinafores of pleats wrapped around dresses," critic Suzy Menkes wrote for the *New York Times* in 2008.

And yet this wasn't the only time Miu Miu played with the apron – or perceived ideas of femininity on the runway. The apron dress appears again and again and again throughout Miu Miu's history. And yet, while total expression of femininity rules in the house of Miu Miu, there's also a carefully studied element of androgyny. Even before Miu Miu started introducing menswear into its collections in 1995, there were clear-cut pieces that could be shared between genders. Like the easy overcoats from Autumn/Winter 2000. Or even the boxy-cut jackets and striped tops.

"I personally have many characters in myself," Miuccia Prada told *Vogue* in 2024, "and I think that many people have different characters in themselves: the feminine part and the masculine part, the gentle and the tough." Likewise, the low-cut, button-down shirts worn open to the navel and tight pants worn on menswear models could have easily been shifted to any of the womenswear models and had the same Miu Miu effect. When Miu Miu wants to be expressly feminine, it is; when it's not, the lines are blurred by thoughtful androgyny.

OPPOSITE Miu Miu reinvented the apron for Spring/Summer 2009, seen here.

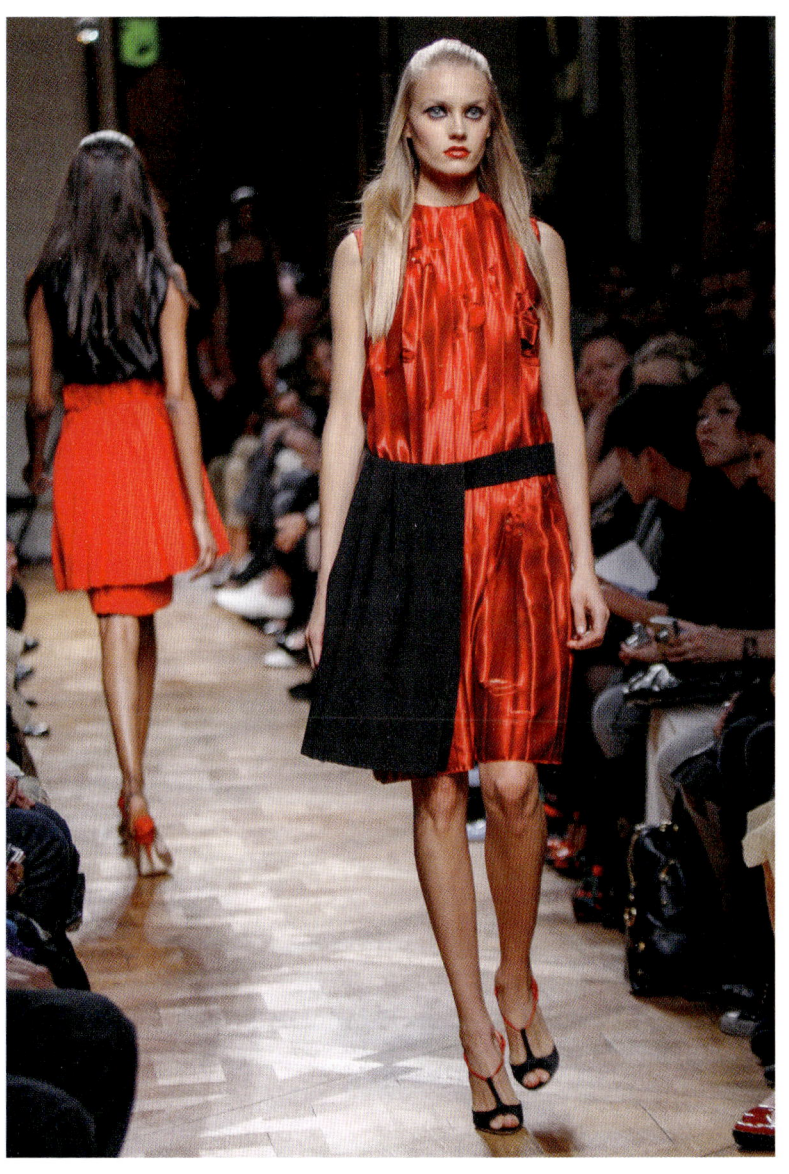

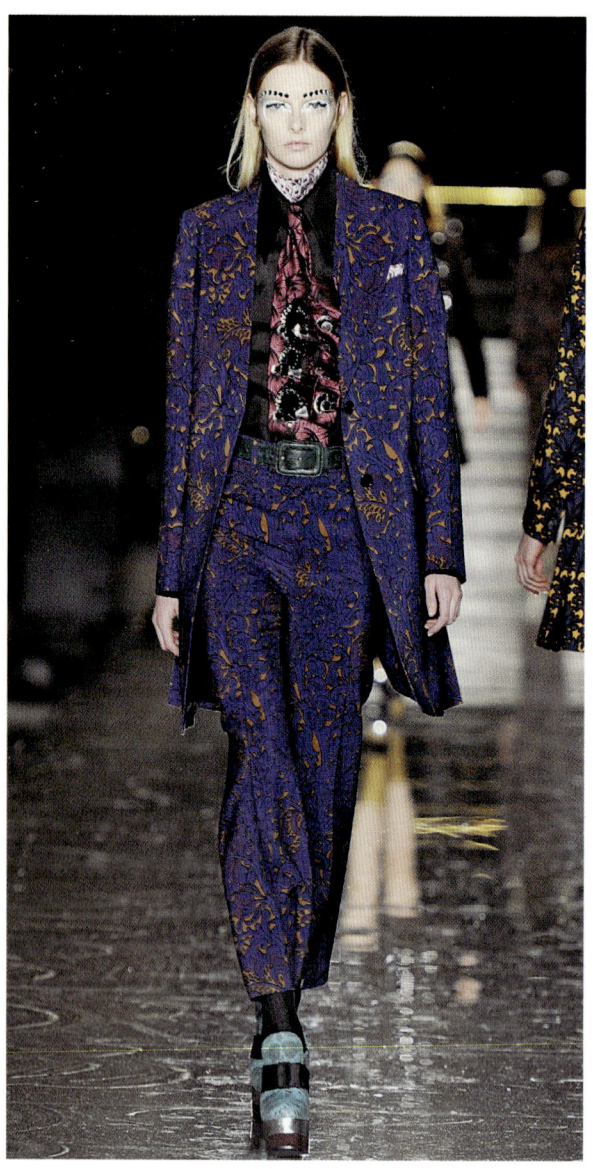

LEFT In the world of Miu Miu, a suit is never just a suit. There is always some element of surprise, like piled-on prints or an embellished tie.

The Uniform

Miuccia Prada undoubtedly plays with the idea of the uniform. Almost every kind of uniform has been touched on – the maid, the office worker, the car mechanic and beyond. The key to making it Miu Miu, of course, is a hefty dose of subversion. You won't see a plain maid's uniform or a mechanic's jacket. Instead, you'll find it covered in floral prints or giant gems, or turned sheer and inside out.

"Firstly, you can hide beneath a uniform, so it's something official that you present, and you don't have to tell anyone anything about yourself. That's probably the most 'serious' reason why I like them. Secondly, because I personally like and respect work and working, when you have a uniform you're generally devoted to a working activity, like all school uniforms, or those of nuns or nurses. For me it's all associated with working, and the declaration of liking what you do at work," she told *System* in 2016. "Actually – and this is probably why I like uniforms in general – very often people are so badly dressed, whereas in a uniform, they are always correct. That's why men always look more elegant, because it's so much easier to be elegant for a man. I would say they look 'proper', whereas for women there are so many choices available that it is much more difficult."

For Miu Miu's debut runway show in New York in 1996, the show notes called uniforms "the most reassuring and elegant dictatorship", adding, "Miu Miu likes discipline and cleanliness of uniforms and she wears them on and off duty in her fantasy world of modern services."

Colour and Print

Even if dubbed a minimal brand from its onset, Miu Miu started playing with colour early on. And did so in a very Miuccia Prada way – putting unexpected, beautifully clashing hues next to one another.

For Autumn/Winter 2002, a tomato-red blazer was styled over a forest green, button-down shirt with burgundy shorts. Little burgundy apron dresses came with neon orange pockets, and the outfit was topped off with a black baseball cap. The

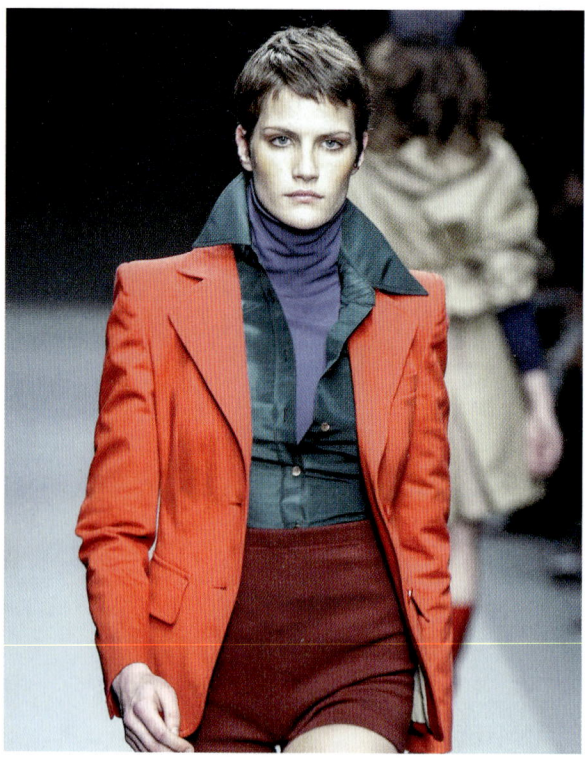

LEFT Miu Miu intentionally clashes colours in unusual ways, seen here for Autumn/ Winter 2002.

Spring/Summer 2003 collection introduced more Technicolour fantasy, featuring a sea of tropical reds, royal purples and saffron yellows, as well as one of the first iconic prints of the brand, a kitschy hibiscus flower done in white on top of bright colours. It was a new sort of take on Hawaiian shirt prints, and a nod to the collective fascination with surf and skate culture at the time. Continuously playing with colour in an unusual way is key and you'll find it in even the most minimalist of Miu Miu collections.

Unexpected, Collectible Accessories and Footwear

"People should express themselves in the way that they want, not follow the clichés of sexiness and beauty – this is my first law," Prada told *W* in 2023. "But I don't want to be the one who promotes this because it's trendy, or to be politically correct." That said, Miu Miu has never played by the rules when it comes to accessories and footwear. A quick scan through previous collections will show you anything from chunky plastic bracelets shaped like apples to sprawling faux fur hats in pink, covered in crystals.

While a brand like Chanel or Celine might show a traditional boater hat, sun hat or a beret, Miu Miu would show a little tailored pinafore dress with an informal baseball cap and then a structured derby hat styled over top of it. For Autumn/Winter 2024, some of the biggest statements of the entire collection were the accessories. The massive gloves that could easily be seen on a construction site or worn by gardeners and the little ladylike pearls had a very specific effect. Without them, the collection would have been a very different story. Paired together with the neon green printed skirts and coral peacoats, it was a tale of originality fuelled by the idea of living various lives.

The footwear from Miu Miu has always been some of the most exciting in the world of fashion. In 2011, the glitter-covered boots with patches of pastel patent leather were everywhere. It was the then equivalent of a viral moment; I remember taping pictures of them to my bedroom walls. Today, the Miu Miu shoes of the 1990s and early 2000s are in high demand, often fetching far more than the original value on secondhand shopping platforms. The shoes back then reflected the signature *ugly chic* dynamic. There were plenty of sneakers that kind of looked like bowling shoes, or boots with square toe shapes and bubble soles for that extra added dose of sporty utilitarianism. The brand's ballet flats and biker boots of the early 2020s also experienced their own viral moments.

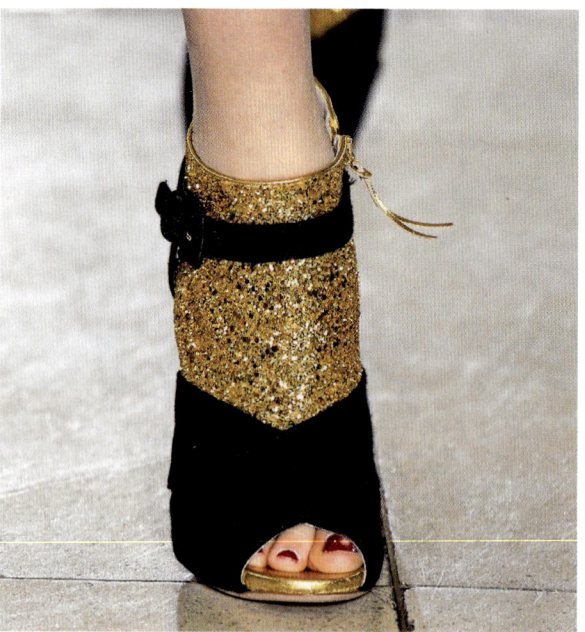

LEFT The iconic glittery peep-toe shoes of the mid-2010s were reposted everywhere on Tumblr and plastered on the walls of aspiring fashion girls.

OPPOSITE Miu Miu takes styling with individuality to an extreme, as seen here with the Derby-inspired hat, contrasting pink bag and heavily embellished dress.

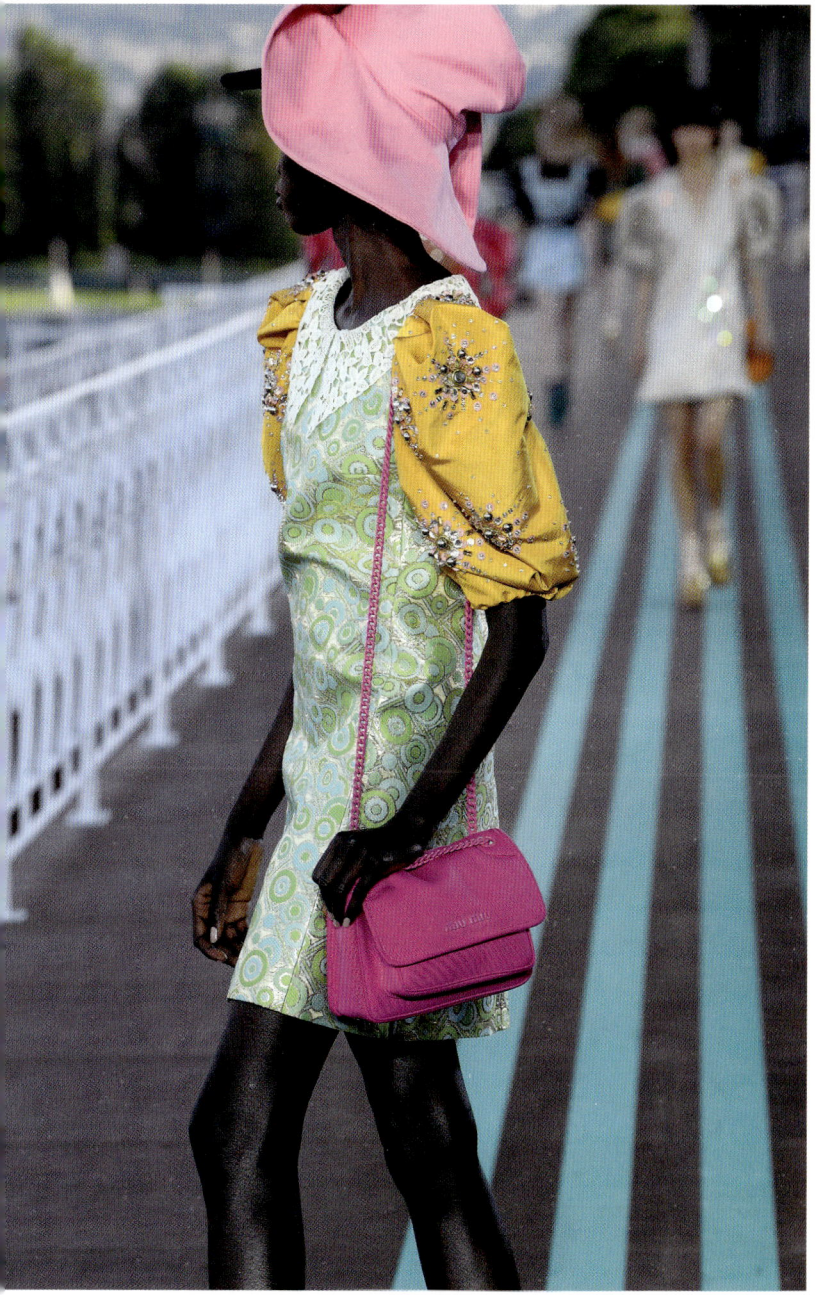

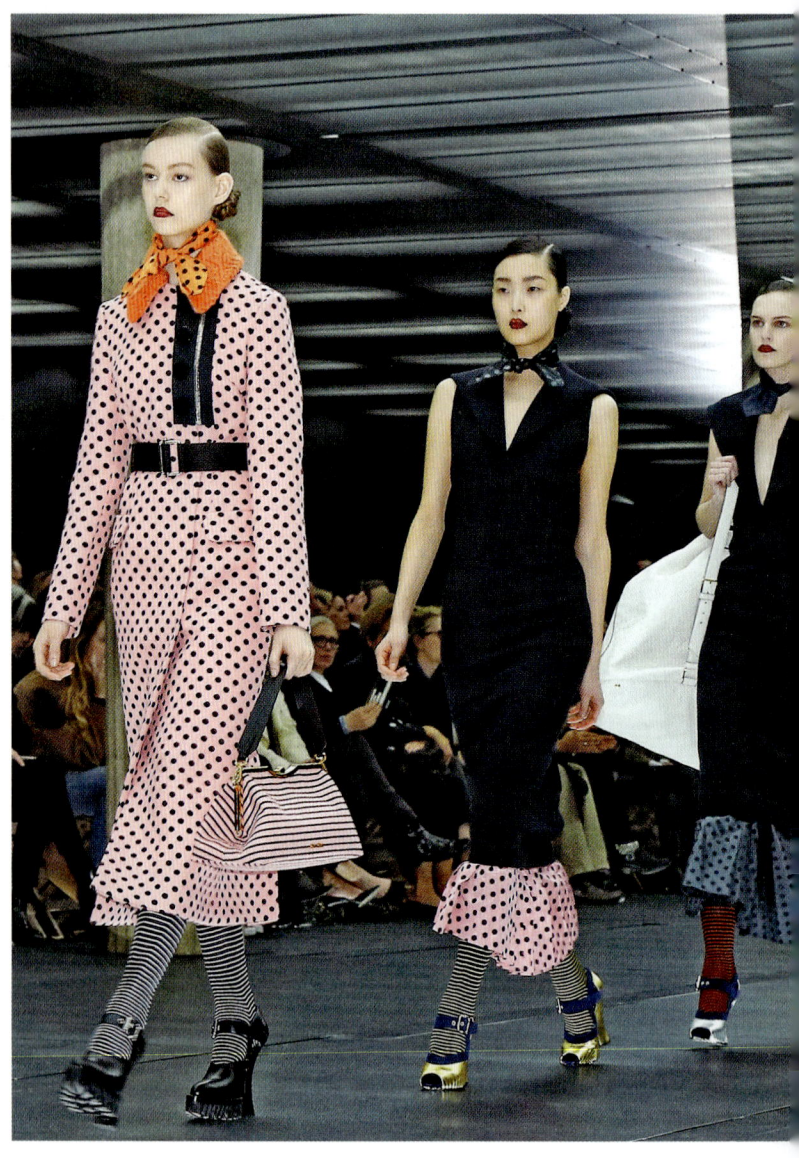

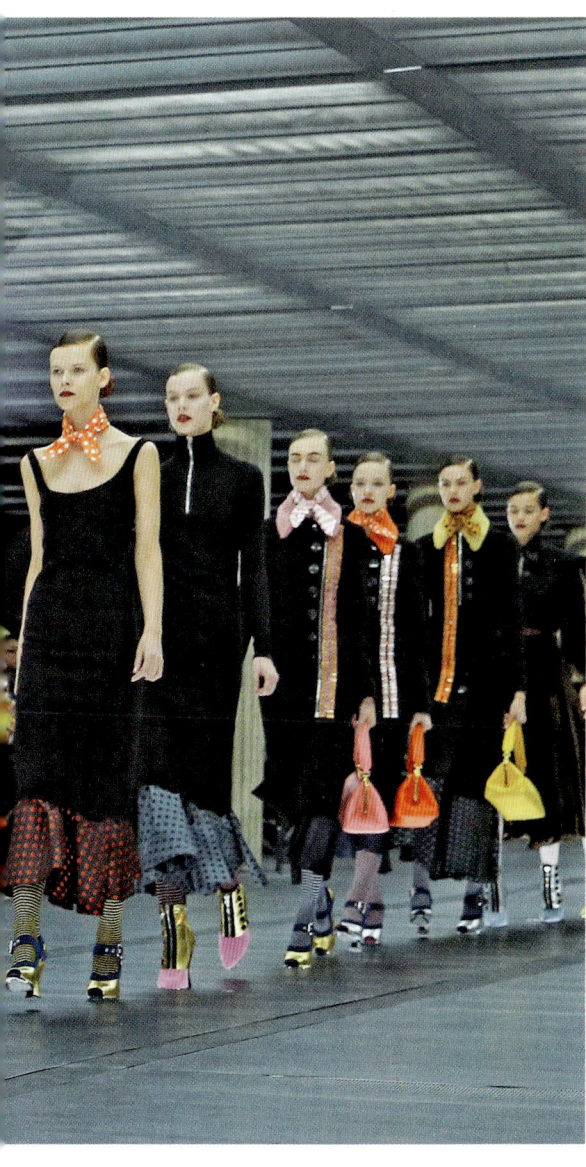

LEFT The Autumn/
Winter 2013
collection showed
a mastery of
outerwear as well as
the brand's unique
take on mixing and
matching subtle
prints.

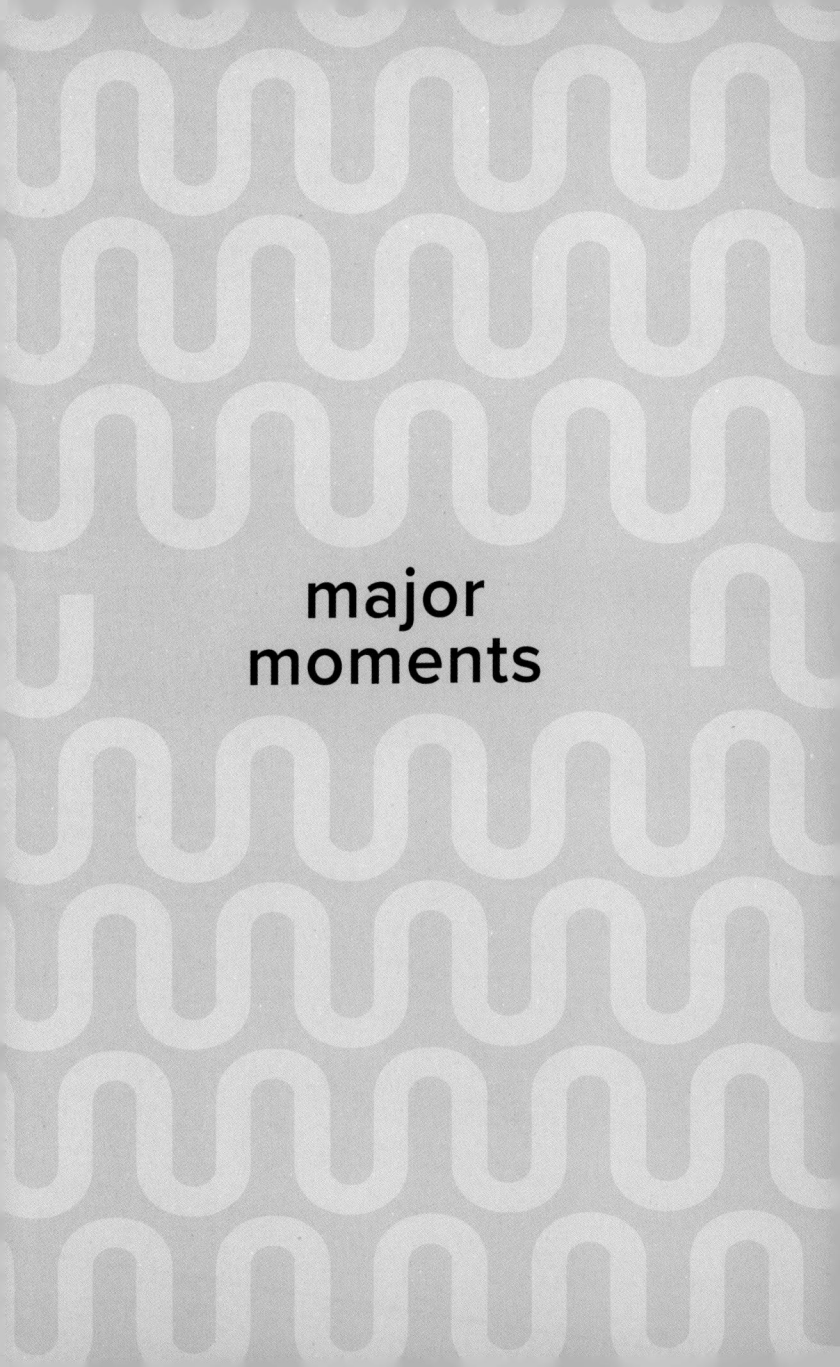

major
moments

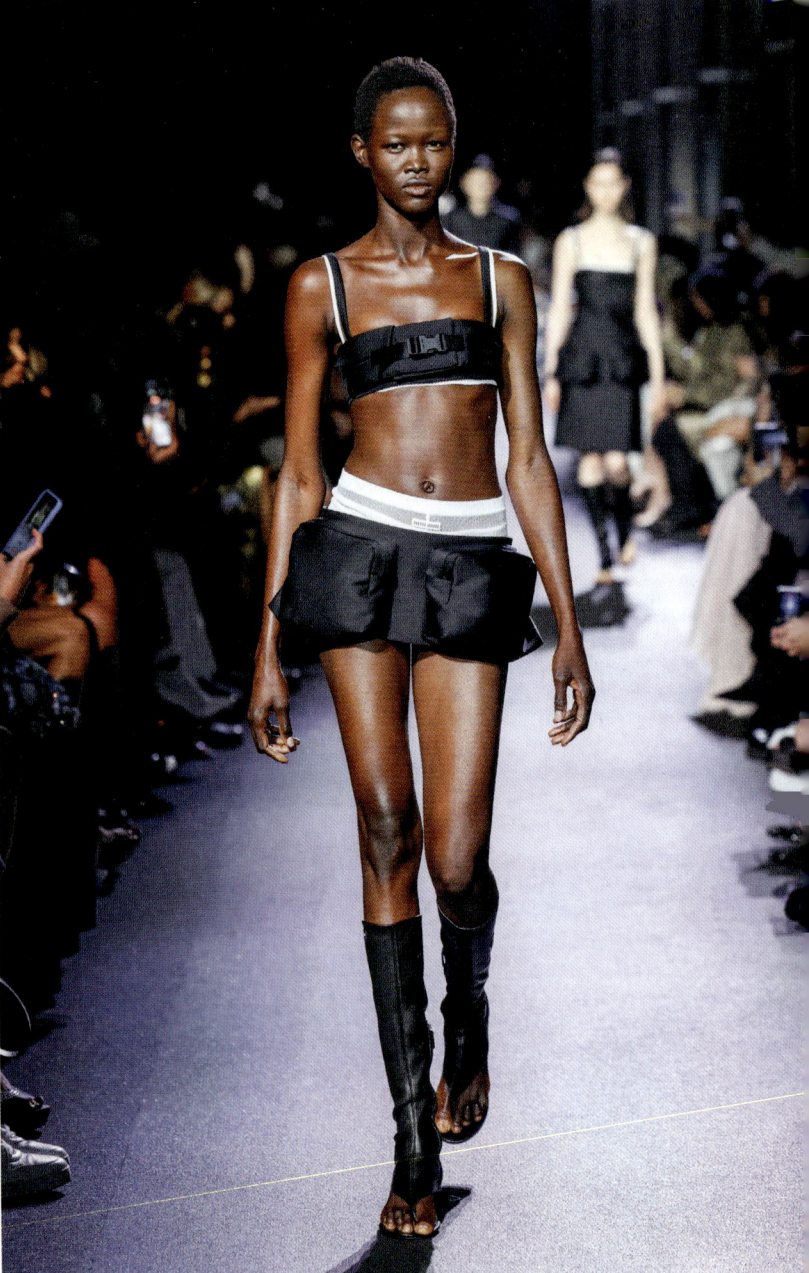

miu miu moments

Miu Miu has always been a brand that knows how to make a splash. Not just visually, but in terms of hot topics too. It makes the world talk. It sparks discourse. It creates trends light years ahead of anything else.

"Miu Miu is romantic but edgy," Claire Danes told the *Evening Standard* from her front-row seat at Miu Miu's Autumn/Winter 1997 show. Miu Miu was founded just three years earlier, and even by that time, Drew Barrymore and Chloë Sevigny were celebrity ambassadors for the brand. Likewise, for Miu Miu's very first runway show (Autumn/Winter 1995), iconic models such as Stella Tennant, Kate Moss and Naomi Campbell walked the runway in New York City's then hub for fashion week: Bryant Park.

The Maximalist Years

After roughly ten years of minimalist-leaning shows with the Miu Miu edge propelled by a quirky point of view on womanhood, Miu Miu shifted gear into a brand that was all about colour, print and excess in embellishment and dressing up. The Spring/Summer 2005 show, for example, was a kaleidoscopic journey through patterns, geometric motifs and girlishness. Models wore mismatched prints and jewelled collars; brightly

OPPOSITE Miu Miu's runway shows today are one of the most anticipated for the industry, always sparking viral moments and setting new trends.

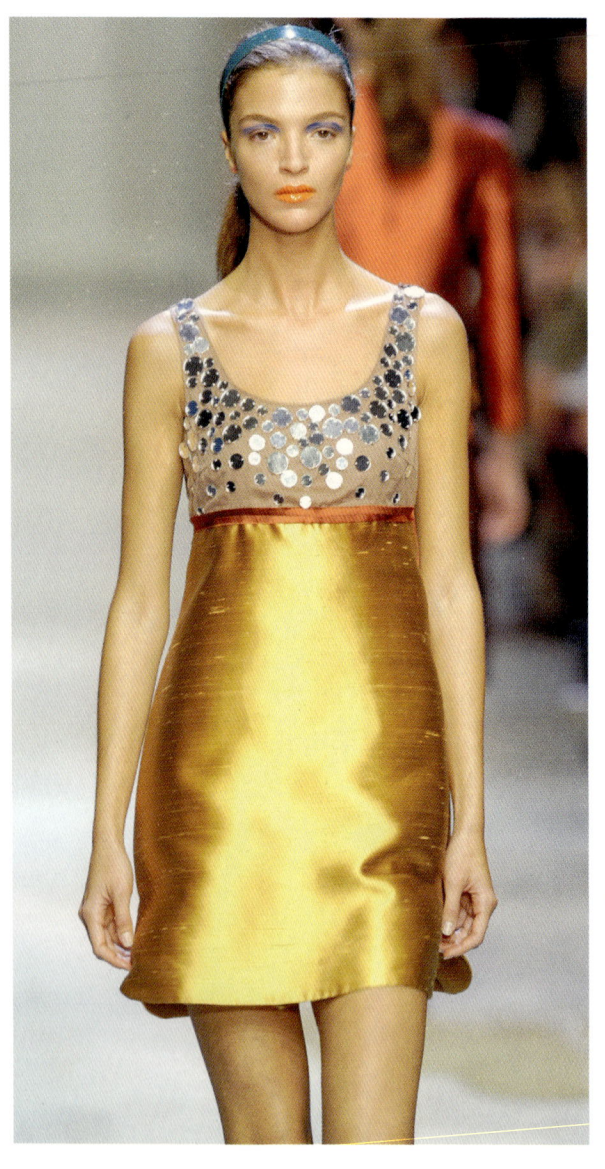

LEFT Embellishment, seen here, is key to the Miu Miu universe.

OPPOSITE The Spring/Summer 2014 collection was full of quirky coats, knitted tights and whimsical accessories.

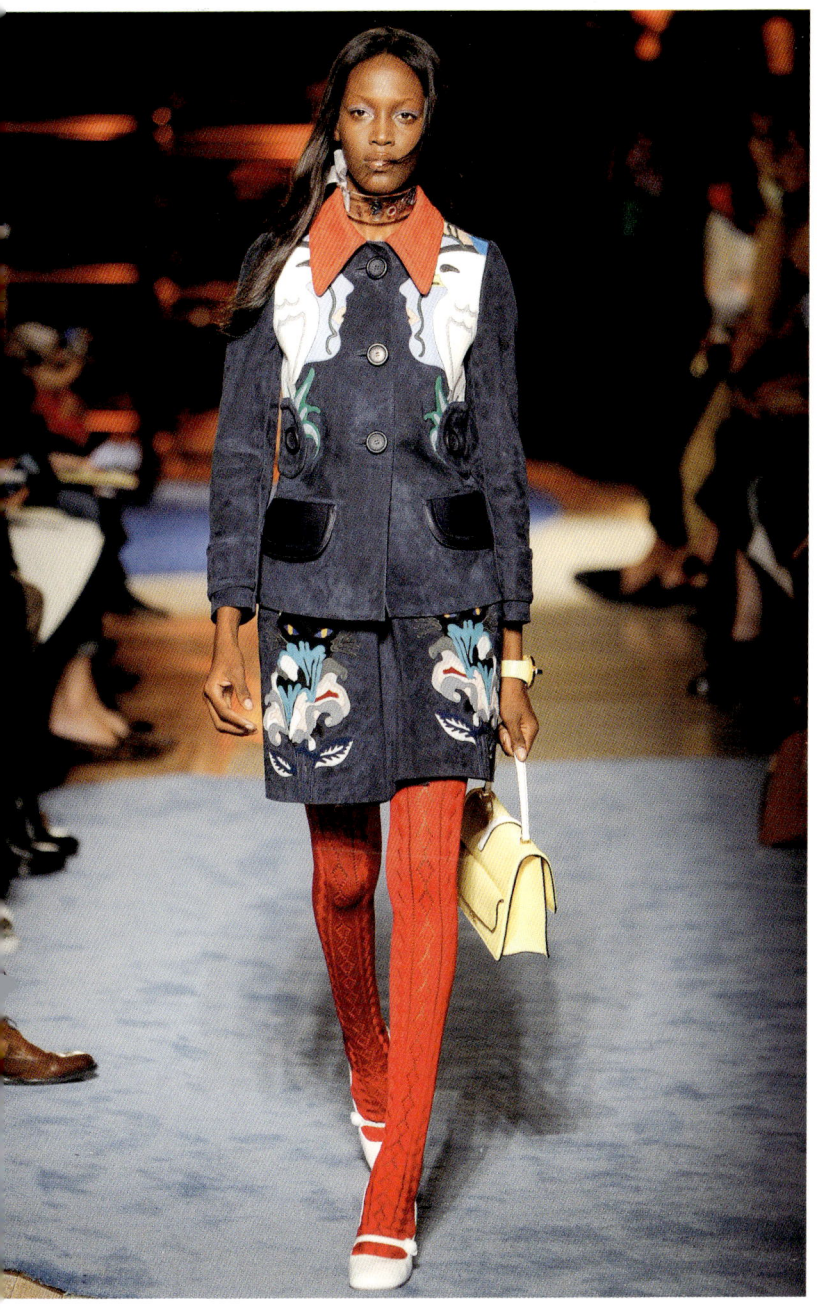

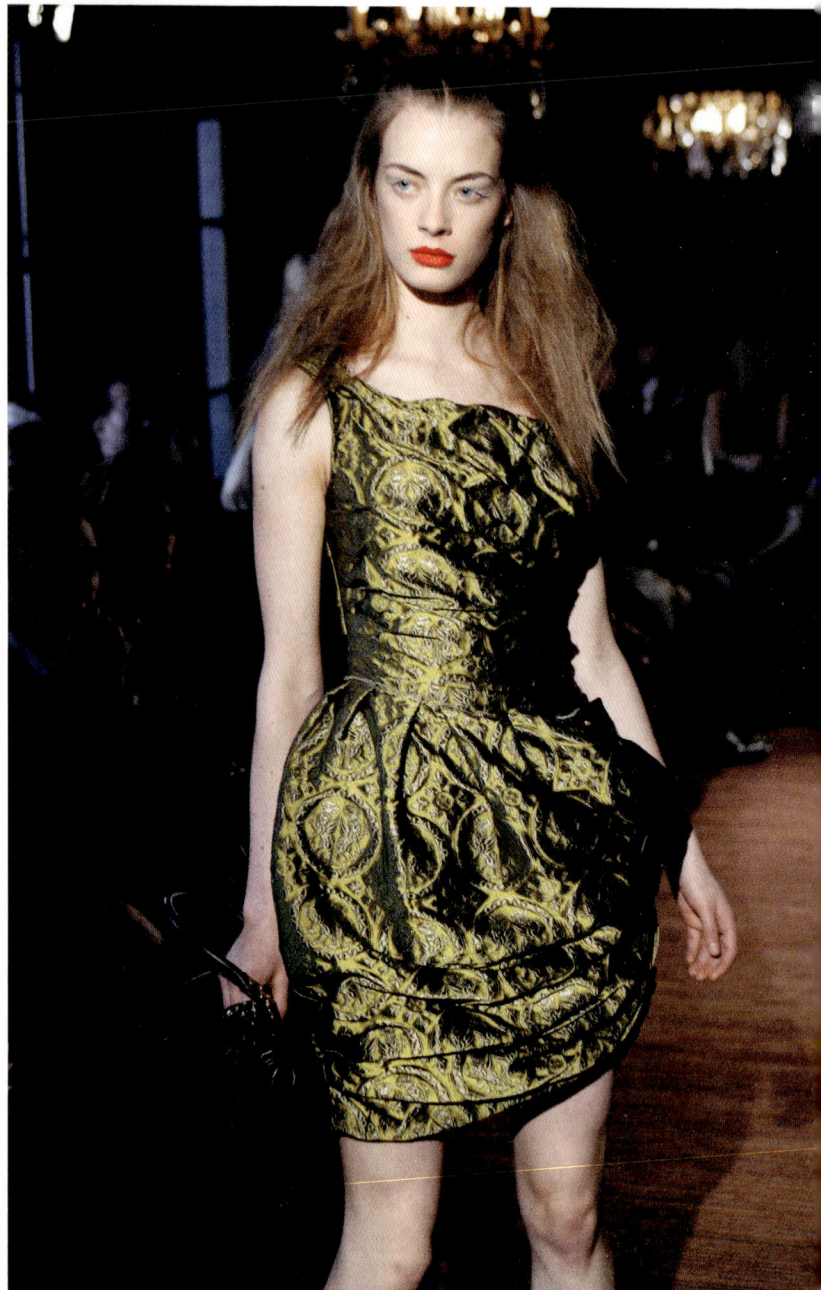

coloured, organically shaped belts; and puffy headbands styled with sunglasses. "Her jewellery-as-embellishment idea is now manifest, at a more accessible price, in the encrusted beaded necklines on dresses and in the panels applied to shantung jackets," the *Vogue* review read. There were chunky necklaces, hoop earrings and massive Mary Poppins-style bags. At this point, even *Vogue* was still referring to the brand as a secondary line of Prada, but it wouldn't be long before things shifted.

"For many, many years, I always wanted to hide my ideas and my personal feelings, my thoughts and my sentiment," Miuccia Prada told *WWD* in 2013. "That was the moment everyone thought Prada was minimal. I never thought it was minimal. For me, it was hiding. But since a few years, I decided I don't want to hide. I think it's necessary to say what you think. It's the most difficult process because you know that you have to give more."

It was the same period of time that Miu Miu made the decision to show its collection in Paris permanently, and with that came a new perspective of sophistication. Take the Autumn/Winter 2006 collection as an example. Shown at the beautifully decorated, famous Left Bank restaurant Lapérouse, models wore jackets with fluffy arms, dark little silk dresses dripping with floral prints and deep red lipstick with white eyelashes. Miu Miu also stepped up its accessories at the time, decorating models in opera gloves, gilded baroque carved wedges and sturdy leather handbags in rich shades of cognac.

Even if the brand seemed to step back from total maximalism for a season, it was all in favour of keeping the house codes. Take, for example, Spring/Summer 2007, when the theme ranged from matronly old lady with thick pleated knee-length skirts to sheer cardigans and matching tops in sickly sweet shades of apricot – both can be seen time and time and time again in Miu Miu collections for the ages.

OPPOSITE Miu Miu began moving in a more maximalist direction in 2006, the same year the brand started showing in Paris, as seen here.

The Spring/Summer 2008 collection was one of the most memorable and celebrated Miu Miu collections of all time. Miuccia Prada was thinking of "life as theater, and all the clichés of how people represent themselves in the world", and sent out clothing that was a reflection of harlequins, ballerinas, French maids and opera attendees. Peplum dresses were covered in rich interpretations of jester figures. Minidresses came cut tightly and with elements of lingerie style, cut low and worn with detached ruffled collars. The accessories themselves were a feast for the eyes – bags made up of leather and exotics shaped into butterflies, or cut-out leather sandal boots that went up to the knees, delicately topped with jewelled dragonflies. Even the most simple of heels were not as they seemed, topped off with little golden handles on the back as if they were precious teacups. This collection is highly celebrated by Miu Miu fans and collectors. Pieces are still in circulation today on the secondhand market and can be seen worn by street style favourites during fashion week.

Cementing itself as the queen of the quirky accessory, Miu Miu sent every single model down the runway for Autumn/Winter 2008 in a skintight hood, ponytails bobbing behind. The looks were composed of heavy cut-out lace and neoprene dresses, each resembling an oddball combination of swimmer's uniform and performer's wear. "I wanted to take sport in a new direction," Miuccia Prada said of the collection backstage.

For Autumn/Winter 2009, the designer interrogated the idea of femmes fatales and what they mean. Beige tailored pieces unfurled into deconstructed looks that were lined with fox fur and exposed the lingerie. It was anything but a conventional sexy look. And the sheer blouses and jewel-encrusted skirts near the end of the runway were satisfyingly Miu Miu-ian.

By the time the Spring/Summer 2010 collection came around, the world was ready for another Miu Miu collection that would

OPPOSITE The iconic Harlequin dress from Spring/Summer 2008.

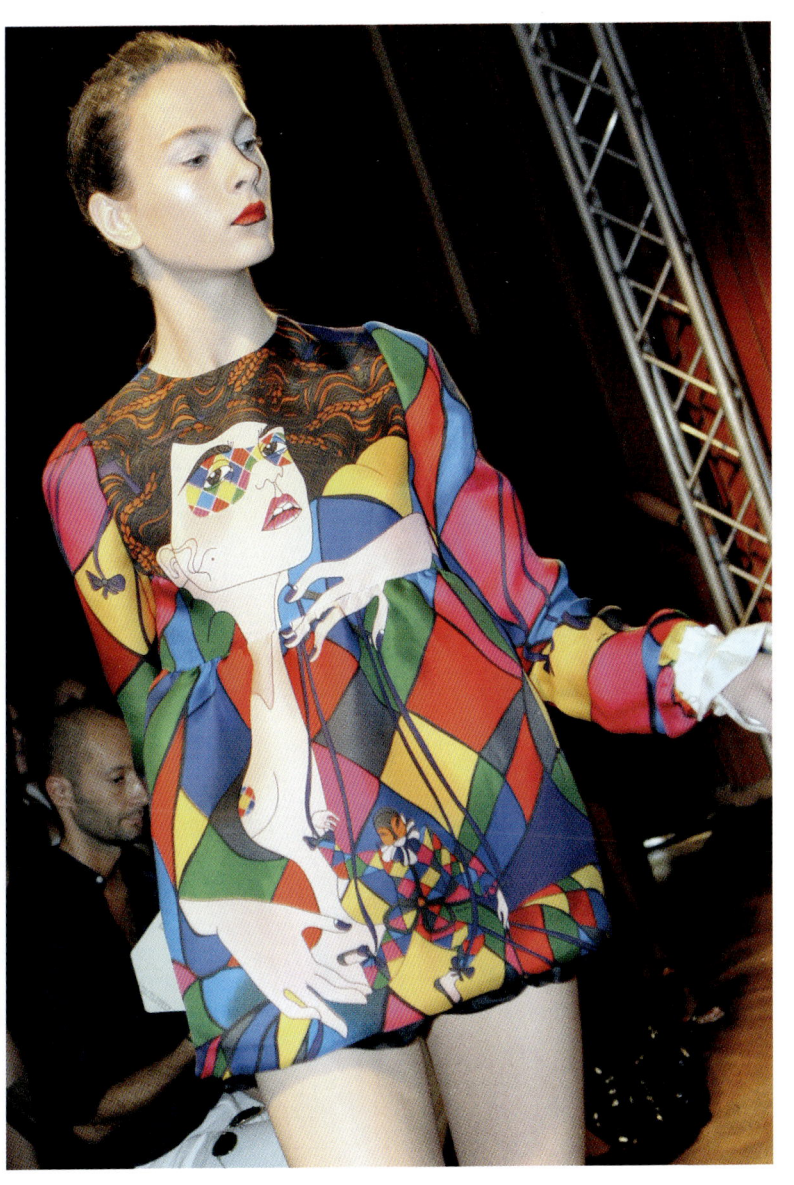

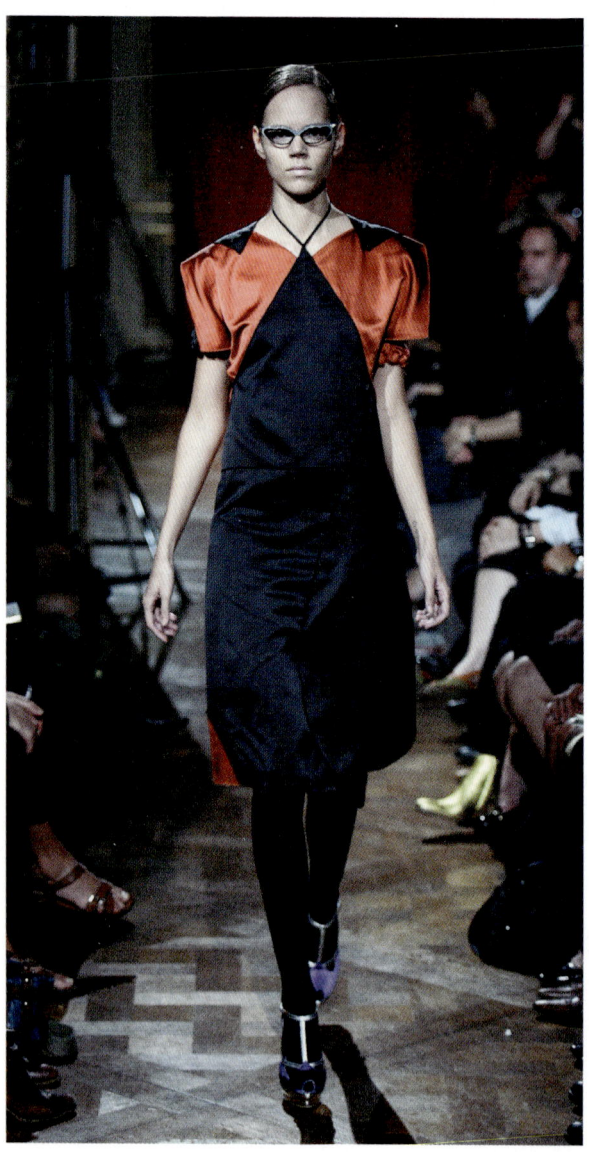

LEFT Miu Miu's runway shows typically showcase unusual eyewear, as seen here.

OPPOSITE The dragonfly boots from Spring/Summer 2008 are legendary among Miu Miu fans.

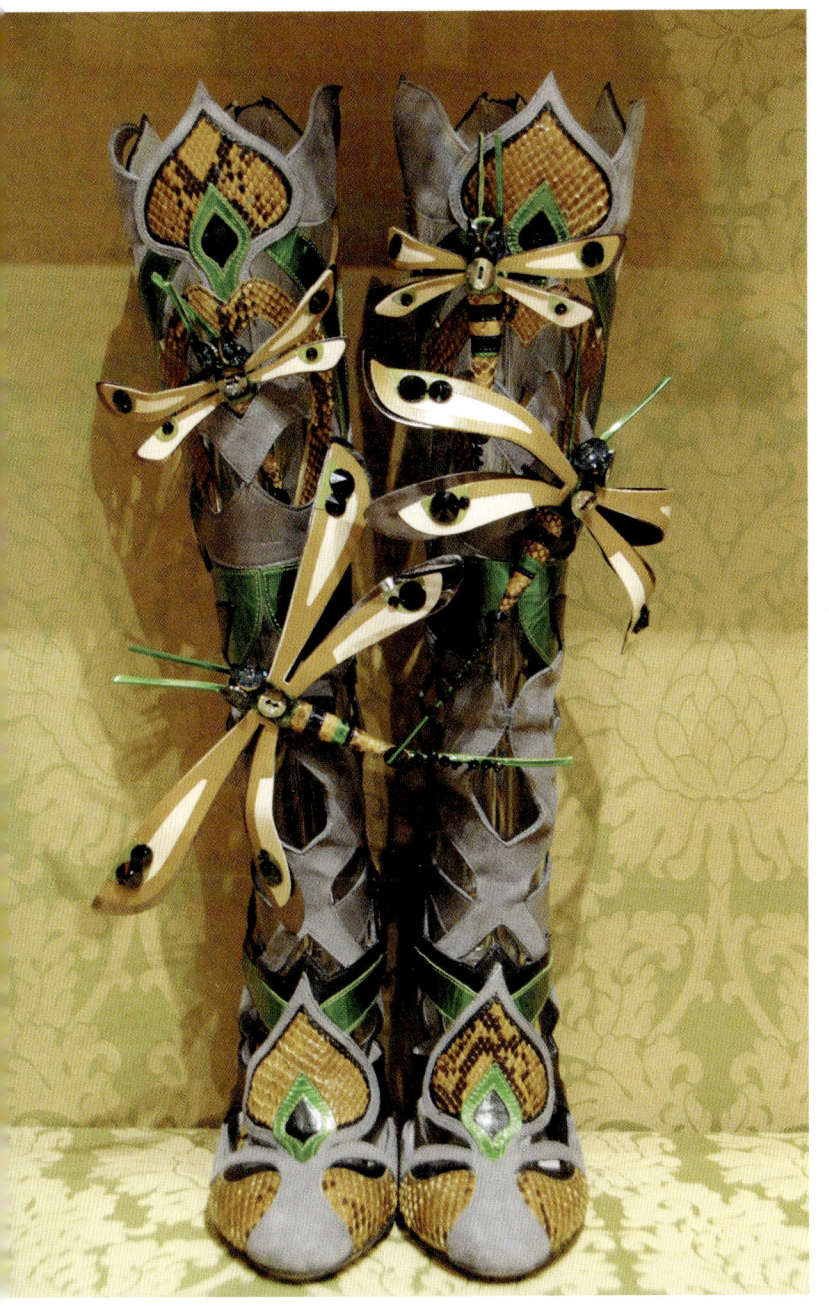

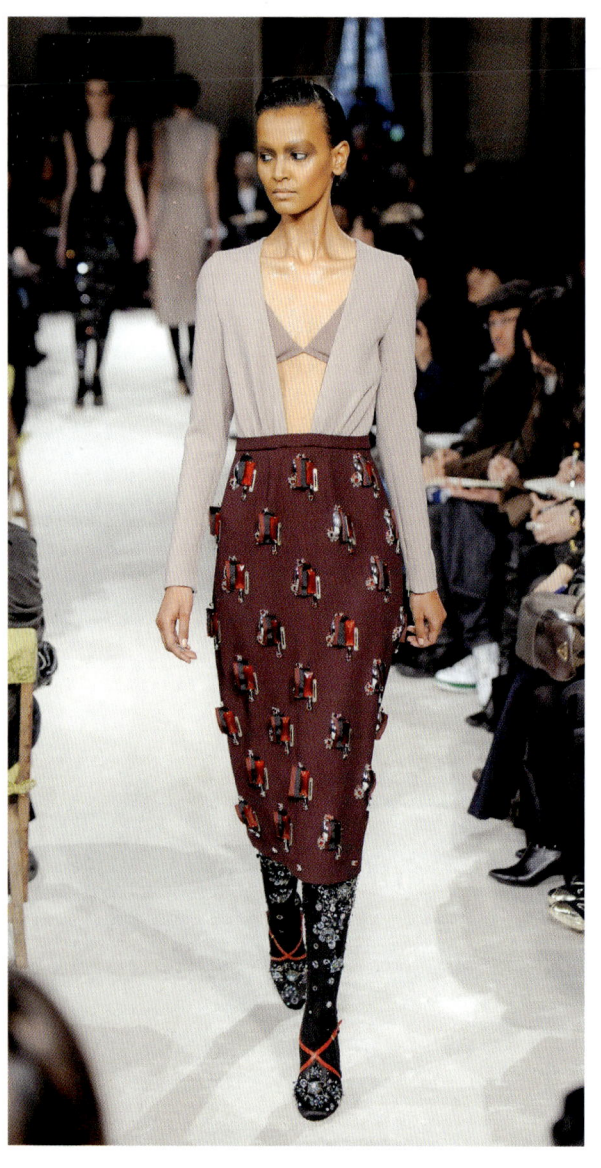

LEFT Miu Miu
Autumn/Winter 2009
played with those
classic elements
of the obscene
and demure; bra
exposure and
embellished midi
skirts.

cement itself as one of the most influential collections for fans and fashion It girls alike. Tailored pantsuits, blouses and skinny trousers were covered in cascades of cats, naked ladies and sparrow prints against serious black, navy and beige backgrounds. Cut-out dresses revealed the space just below the bust and were covered in hundreds of sequins and crystals. Loose bloomers with cats all over were juxtaposed with those tailored gem-encrusted tops. With hair braided and down past the waist, it was the total embodiment of the Miu Miu moment. Collectors still search for these pieces and value them today. "I was questioning innocence, questioning

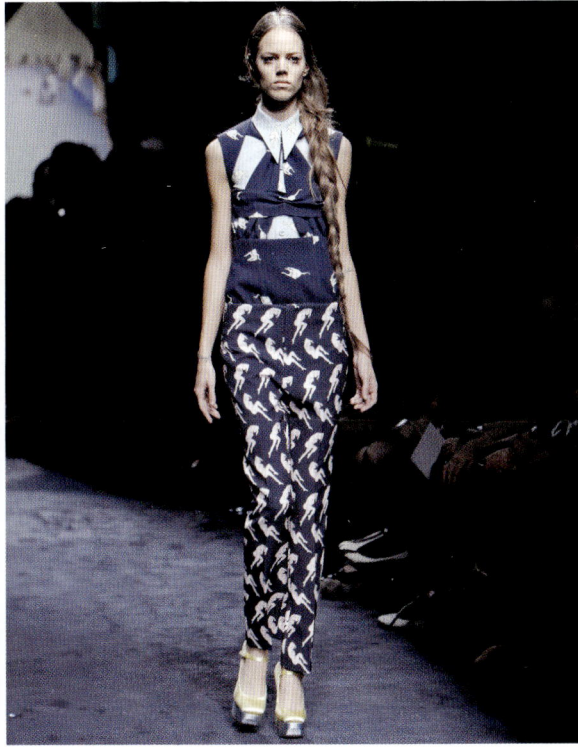

LEFT For fans of the brand, Spring/ Summer 2010 is another iconic collection. The cat, sparrow and naked lady prints would later be revisited.

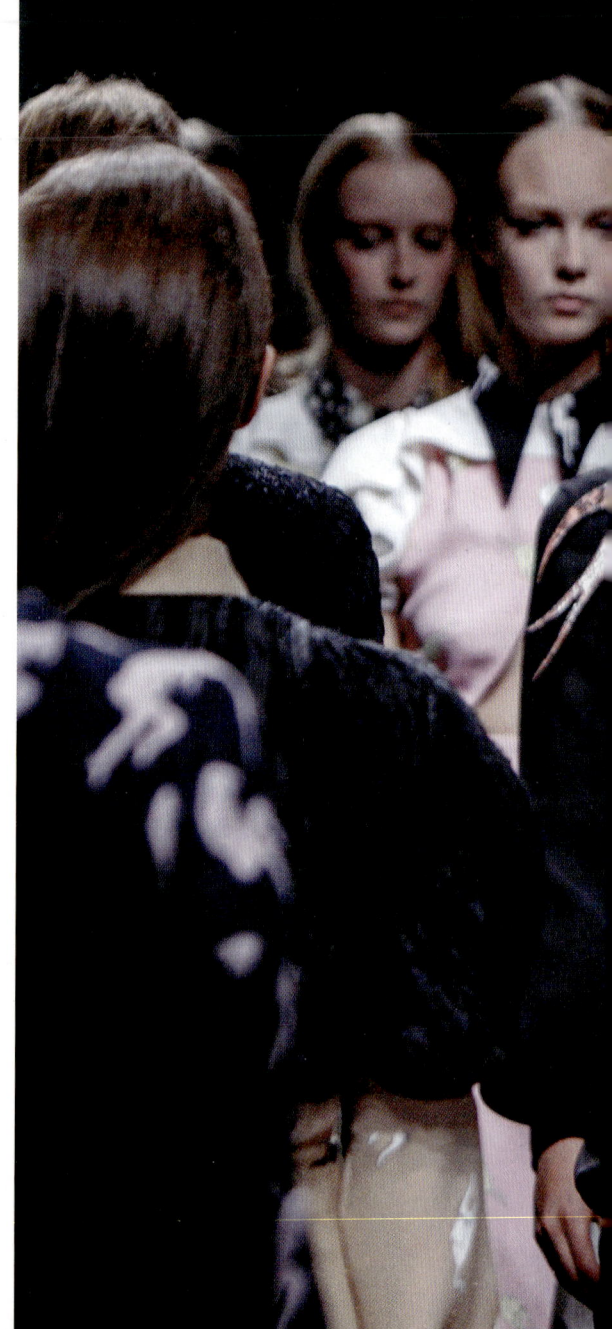

RIGHT For Spring/
Summer 2010,
Miu Miu mixed
whimsical prints
and overloaded
embellishment
for a magical
wonderland feel.

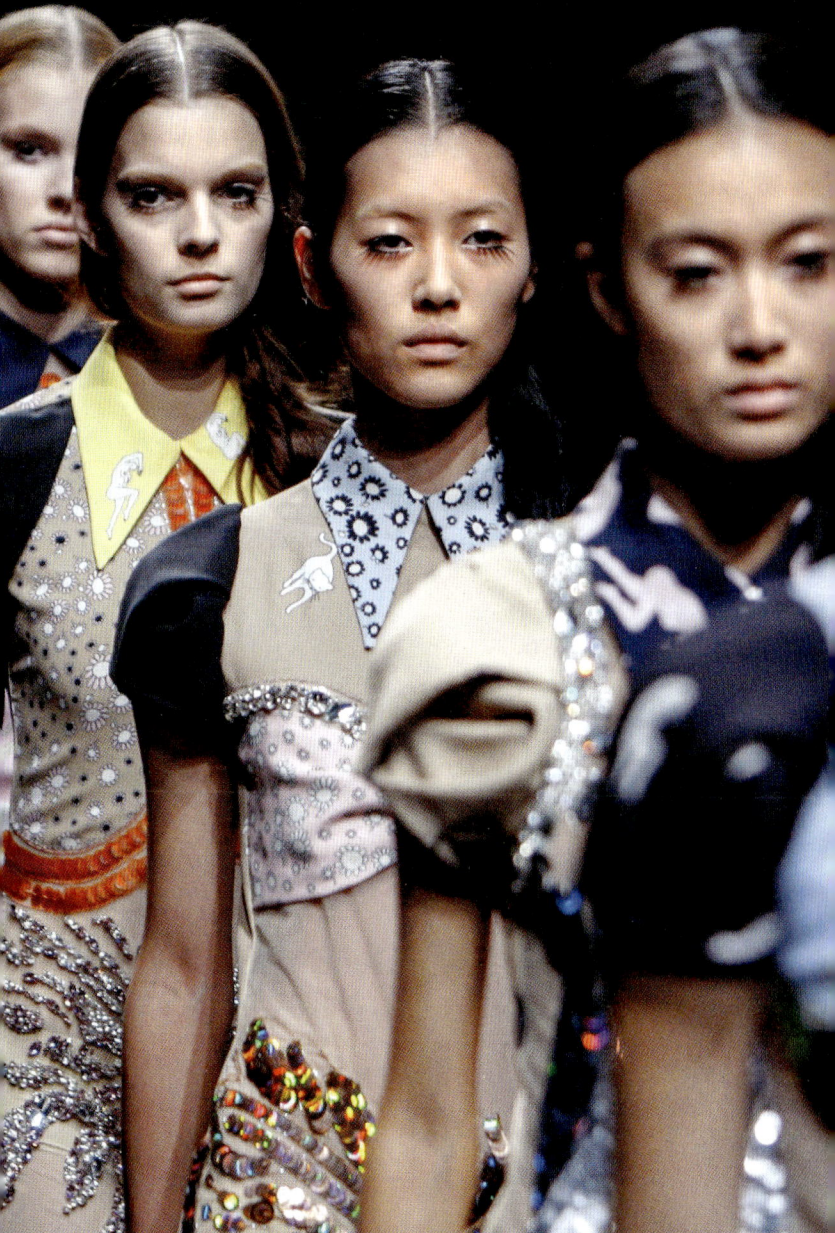

youth," Miuccia Prada said backstage. "What do they mean today in a world that's the opposite?"

The Spring/Summer 2011 collection ushered in Miu Miu's great era of statement outerwear. Models wore leather jackets outlined in colourful appliqué that could have been Scandinavian or American Western – one couldn't really put a place or date on them – and that's part of what made them so incredible. Now highly sought-after by collectors, these jackets go for much more on the secondhand market than their original price. The rest of the collection was full of whimsical prints of stars, swans and flowers. "I was thinking

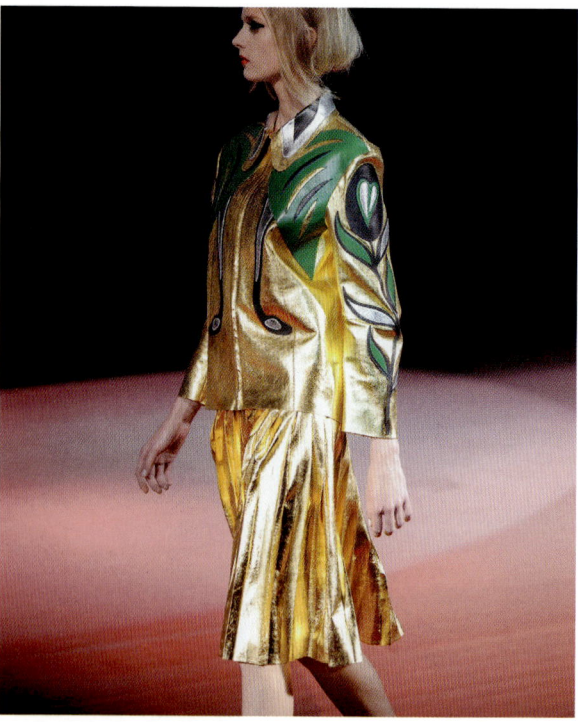

LEFT The outerwear from Spring/Summer 2011 will always be remembered for its unusual colour combinations and embellishments.

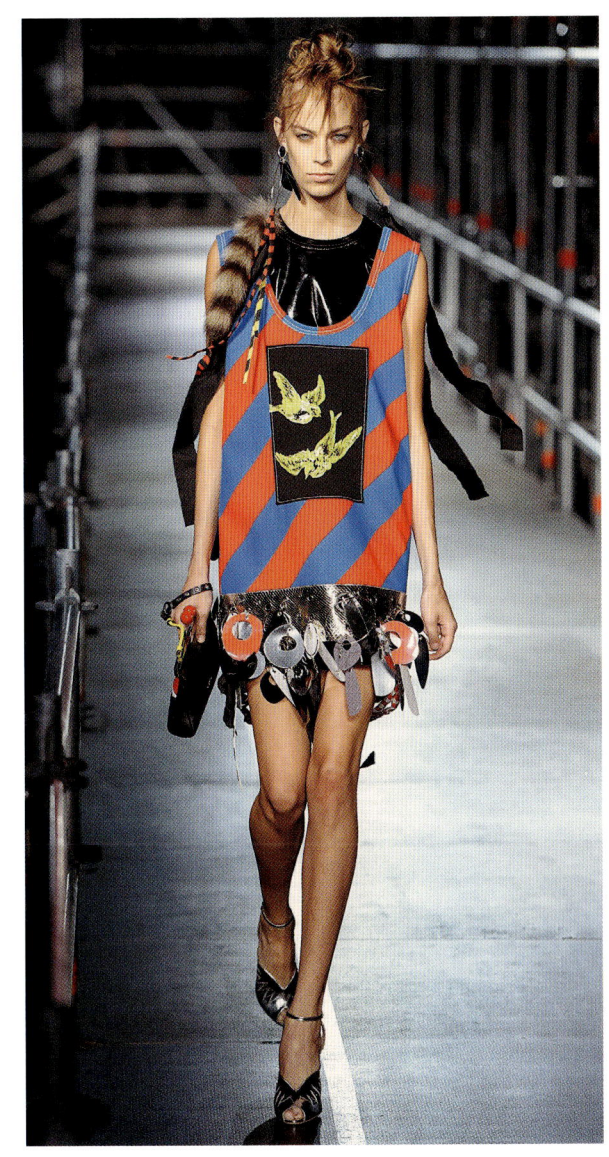

RIGHT Miu Miu Resort collections of the past have been some of the most extreme and expressive, as seen here with Resort 2016.

about everybody's obsession with being famous," Miuccia Prada said of the collection.

The Miu Miu of the mid 2010s was all about over-the-top accessorizing, and no other collection could have proved that as much as Resort 2012. Wearing a slew of lace and preppy looks dotted in gingham, there were crystal headbands, piles of pearl necklaces and heart-shaped bracelets. They came with a particularly '80s feeling. The message was clear: more is more. Continuing the commitment to out-of-this-world outerwear, the Autumn/Winter 2013 show doubled down on coats in poppy pink polka dots, or in bright yellow with pink fur collars. Worn with long striped socks, they added a surreally whimsical element that toyed with the designer's forever fascination with girlhood on the brink of womanhood. Spring/Summer 2014 was full of outerwear that was over the top and unlike any other designer collection out there at the time. Pastel combinations joined forces for coats that looked like new versions of '60s mod silhouettes, and leather and wool options covered in geometric black cats were some of the brand's most memorable designs of all time. Autumn/Winter 2014 followed suit, with pastel quilted hooded jackets, curly black and white furs, and juicy translucent raincoats in stiff fabrications. Key to the Miu Miu style was layering – adding more, more, more – and then juxtaposition. A shining tinsel coat with a utilitarian nylon hood, for example.

Around this time, nothing was off limits for Miu Miu. The Resort 2015 collection played with brightly coloured crochet pieces and outerwear that was completely entrenched in psychedelic swirls. With messy hair and gladiator sandals, the look was iconically strong and full of personality. Autumn/Winter 2015 experimented with ladylike elegance and glamour, offering croc-embossed coats in rich shades of cherry red and

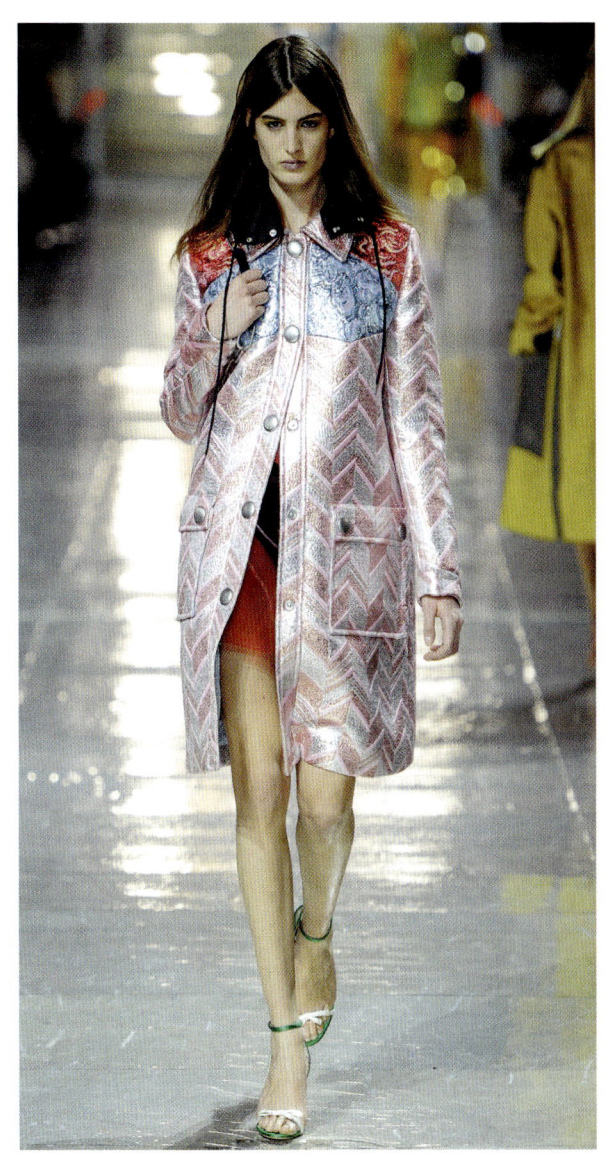

RIGHT Miu Miu's
Autumn/Winter 2014
collection went all
out with glittery,
colourful outerwear.

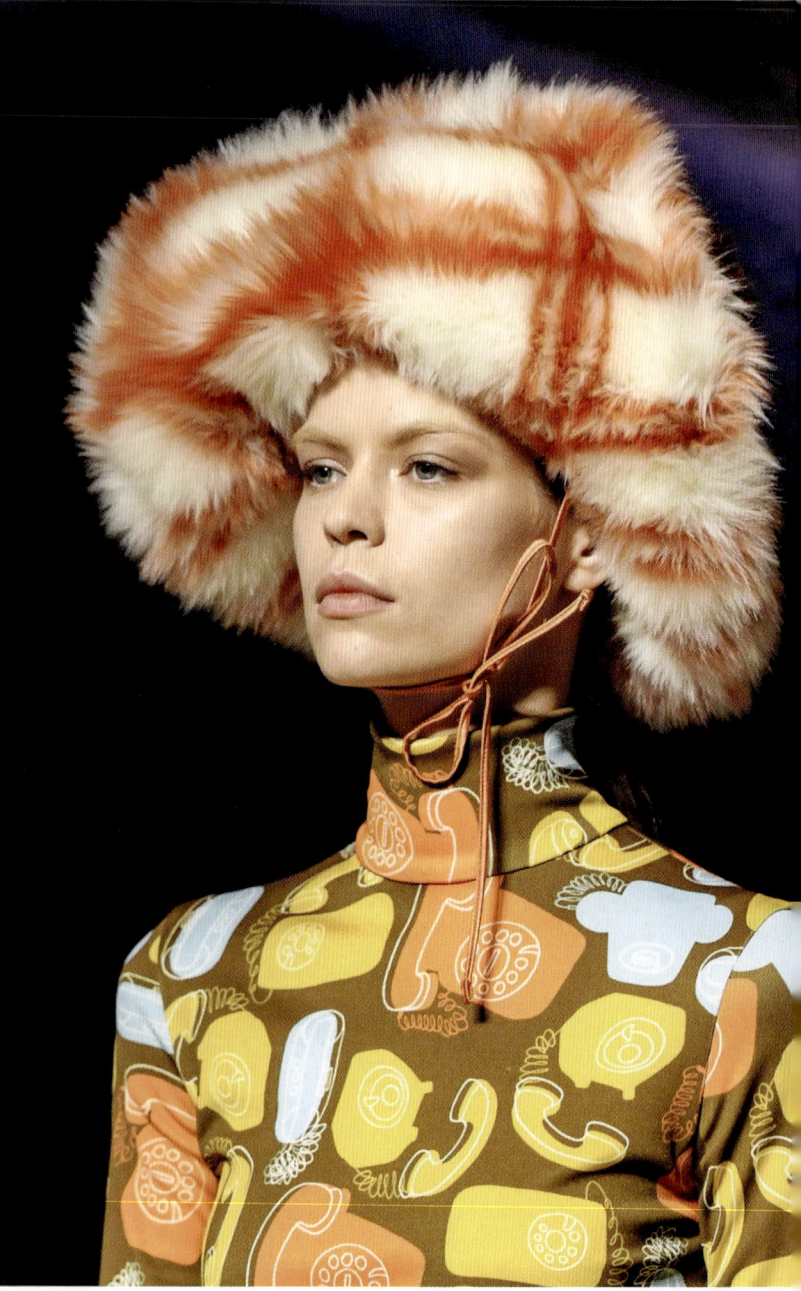

orange, layered over striped tops and miniskirts, of course, and with lots of crystal flower jewellery. Much like the rest of Miu Miu's historic collections, the range defied eras and age.

The 2016 Resort collection brought back several of the Miu Miu symbols, like cats and sparrows, and mixed them into baggy sheer dresses and put them on Technicolour heeled cowboy boots. And Autumn/Winter 2016 took mechanic-like jackets and turned them on their head with lush velvet fabrics, ironic name patches and pearls and beading embroidery. Along with that came full-length ball skirts in delicate shades of lilac and raspberry. It was a study of beautiful contradictions, rooted in the careful idealism of Miu Miu. "Nobility and misery!" exclaimed Miuccia Prada.

The designer again touched on the concept of the swimmer and pin-up for Spring/Summer 2017. Models wore flowering swim caps, little halterneck tops and swimsuits with boldly printed, 1970s-style terrycloth coats belted over them. Like much of the intrinsically out-there Miu Miu outerwear that came before this, there was, of course, a twist. Like luscious fur collars and beaded embroidery lining the front panels of the designs. In terms of shoes, some of the most extreme options yet were presented: towering translucent jelly platforms shaped like three-dimensional waves and topped with flowers. On the opposite end of the spectrum, there were flat pool slides with patent leather blossoms on top.

Taking outerwear to the pinnacle of extremes, Miu Miu's Autumn/Winter 2017 collection may have been its most over the top yet. There were all sorts of chunky faux furs in bright, lucid colours – coral, lilac, kelly green, butter yellow, and big, hulking fluffy boots and matching massive hats to match. Plus, the occasional monster-sized mitten or two. On top of all this was crystal jewellery, sparkling belts

OPPOSITE Autumn/ Winter 2017 will always be recognized as one of the most expressive Miu Miu collections of all time, with extreme accessories and playful prints.

OVERLEAF More looks from Autumn/ Winter 2017, full of references to the 1920s and hip-hop, turned on their head.

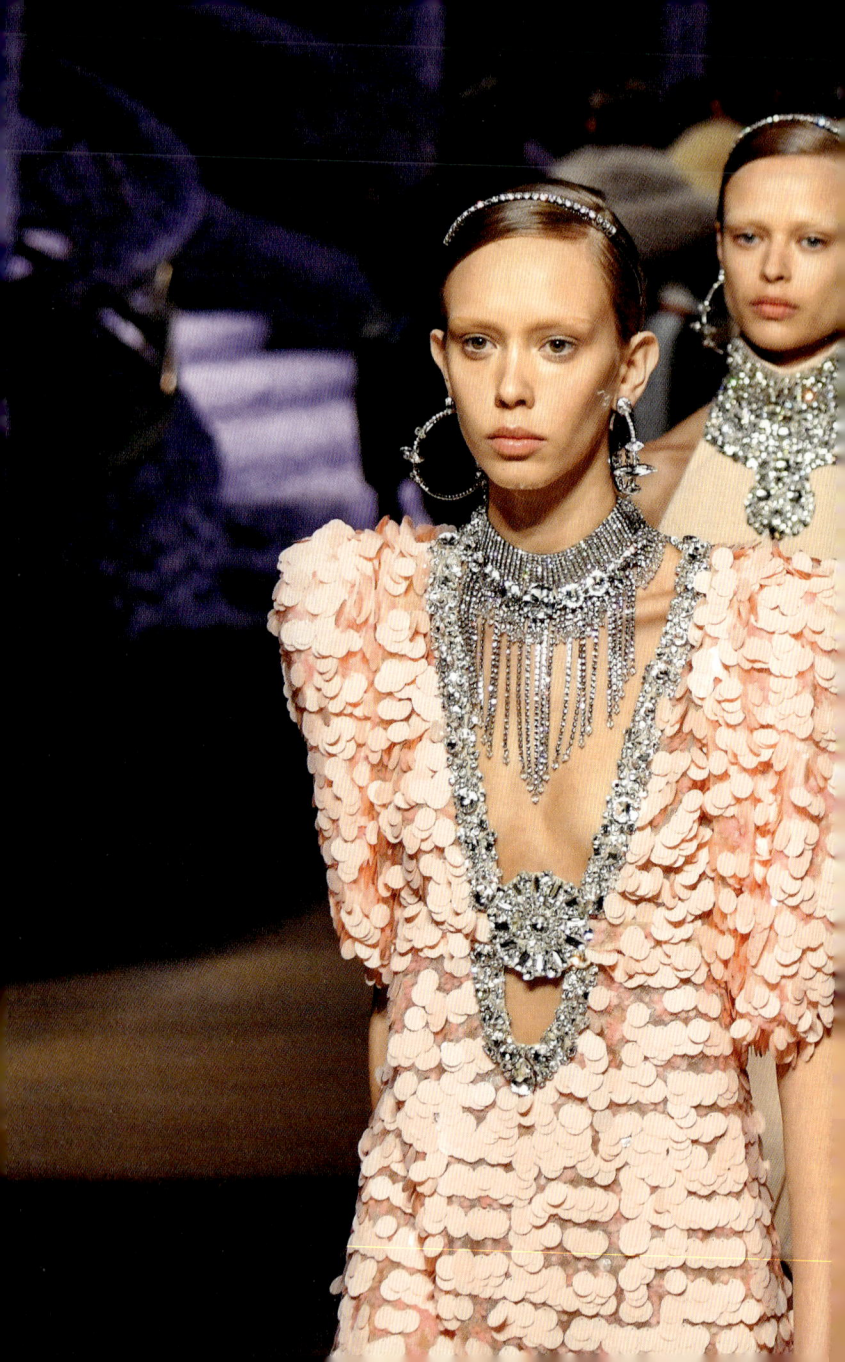

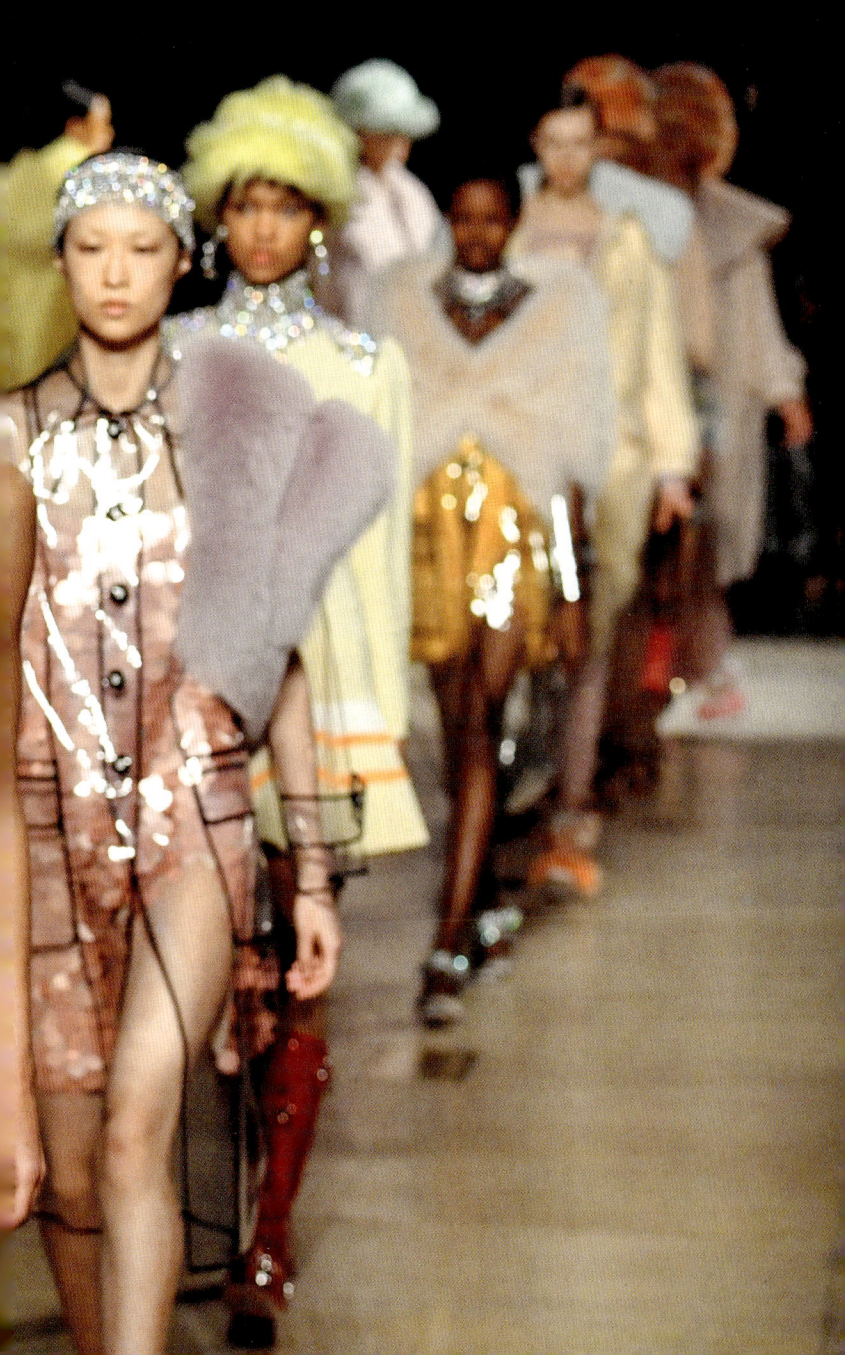

and Hollywood-ready glittering sunglasses. When the whole look wasn't just outerwear, it was wool pants and dresses and skirts, printed with retro-looking telephones, birds and cats (the latter two are favourites of the designer). "It's about the madness of glamour, in front of an uncertain future," she said, and then added, "and I am getting really interested in so many kinds of beauty."

The Autumn/Winter 2019 collection was one of Miu Miu's last maximalist collections before diverting back to the minimalist era that started it all. In the darkened show venue, sheer embellished dresses that looked like they took some influence from the 1920s and 1930s were shown alongside camouflage shearlings. Floral printed nylon capes with cargo pockets and frilled black tulle skirts brought forward a feeling of forest goth. The Resort 2020 collection also took a lot of influence from vintage silhouettes, but that has always been slightly intentional at Miu Miu. Miuccia Prada herself has been known to frequent vintage stores, such as Didier Ludot in Paris, which she often visited with her friend and collaborator, Manuela Pavesi (who passed away in 2015). "Manuela Pavesi was the most stylish woman I have ever known," Ludot told the *New York Times*. "She'd arrive with diamonds in her hair, wearing a fur coat over a pair of men's pajamas and men's Westons. She once bought some vinyl Courrèges pieces from me with crocodile skin print. At the next Prada catwalk collection, there they were! It's not that they copy or imitate. They inspire themselves with the best of what they find here."

Resort 2020 was shown outdoors in Paris at a horse racetrack, the models wearing extreme versions of 1940s silhouettes: collared slouchy dresses with puff sleeves covered in horses, or paperbag waist shorts, with chic leather skirts and polos and large derby-style hats thrown over baseball caps.

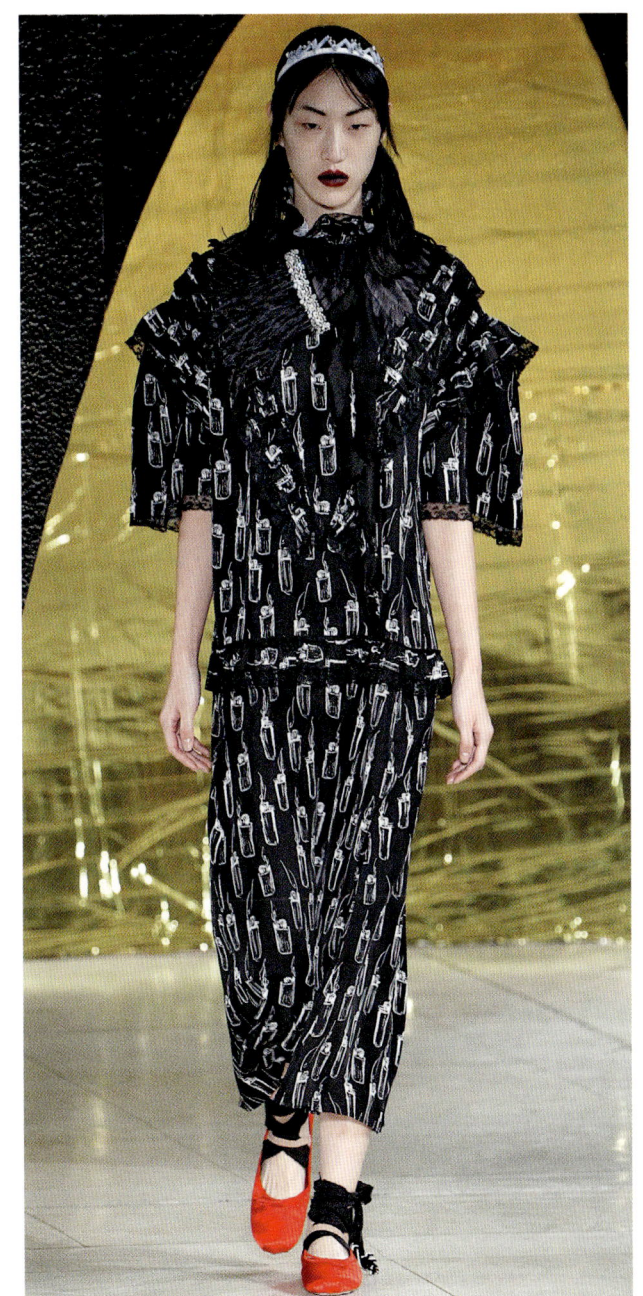

RIGHT The Spring/ Summer 2016 collection had elements of goth ballerina, with some models sporting tiaras.

The Ballet Flats

Miu Miu has been one of the most interesting brands in terms of footwear, often producing boundary-breaking styles that skirt the line between extremely utilitarian and incredibly impractical. But perhaps no Miu Miu shoe has been as famous as the ballet flat. The brand has long been a fan of flat shoes, but for the Autumn/Winter 2016 show, ballet flats balanced out goth rock chic Victorian sleep-like dresses printed with candles and sheer little tulle peignoirs.

Presented as a simple little flat with two Mary Jane straps going across the tops, the shoes came with black and white gingham wrap ribbon ankle straps. When the style was first released, it was popular, but no one could have expected that it would be one of the brand's most well-known shoes to date.

Miu Miu re-released their iconic ballet flats in 2022, this time without the black leather Mary Jane straps and with a ballet-inspired piece of elastic in its place. For the Autumn/Winter 2022 show, the models wore them on the runway with long, scrunched-up socks, perfectly timed to the cultural phenomenon that became obsessed with "balletcore", or rather, the aesthetic of all things ballet-inspired. The brand also released a satin, high-heel version, and even debuted a new take on the original double-strap version in 2024.

In 2022, the global shopping and data platform Lyst named Miu Miu ballet flats as the number one most searched product for Q3. From Katie Holmes to Rosalía and Alexa Chung, so many celebs wore them that it's impossible to count.

OPPOSITE Miu Miu's ballet flats have proven to be a huge commercial success, with people of all different aesthetics wearing them.

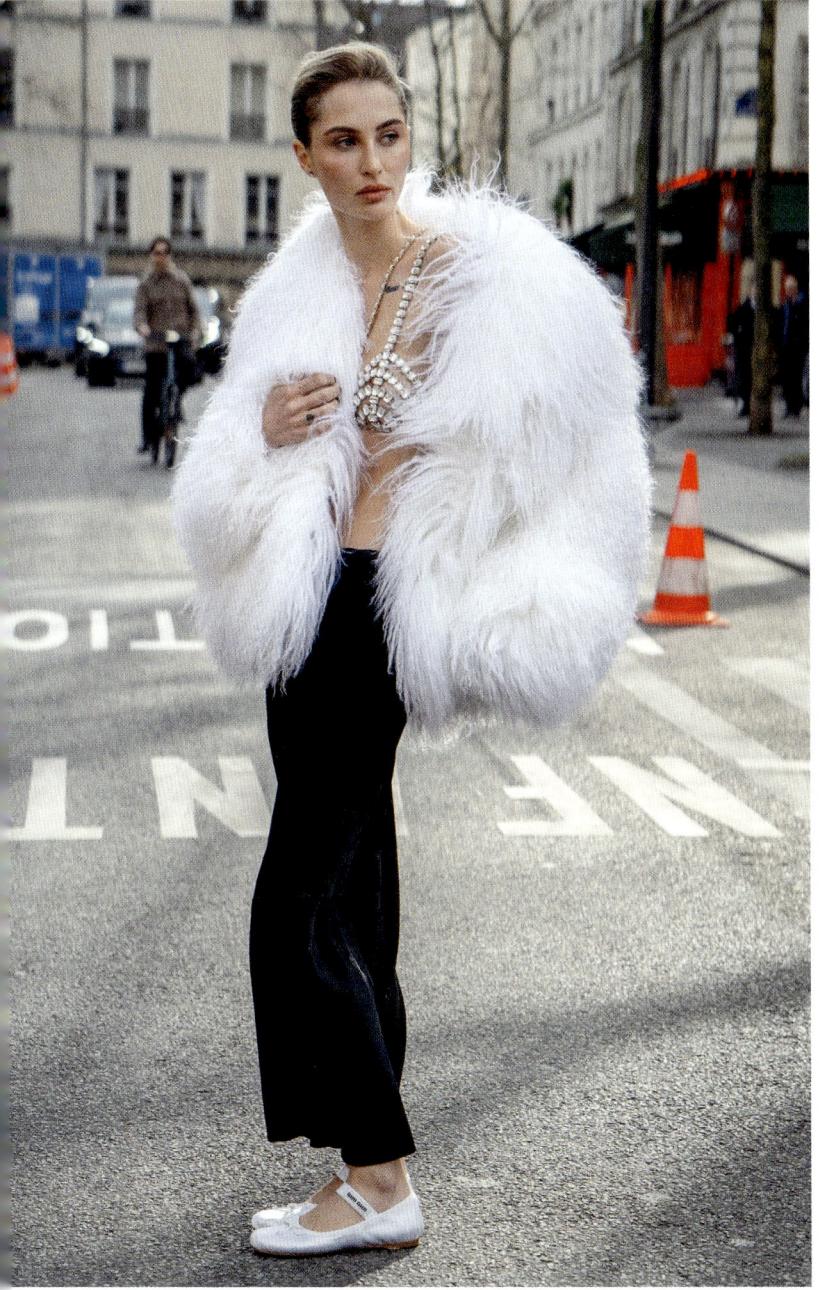

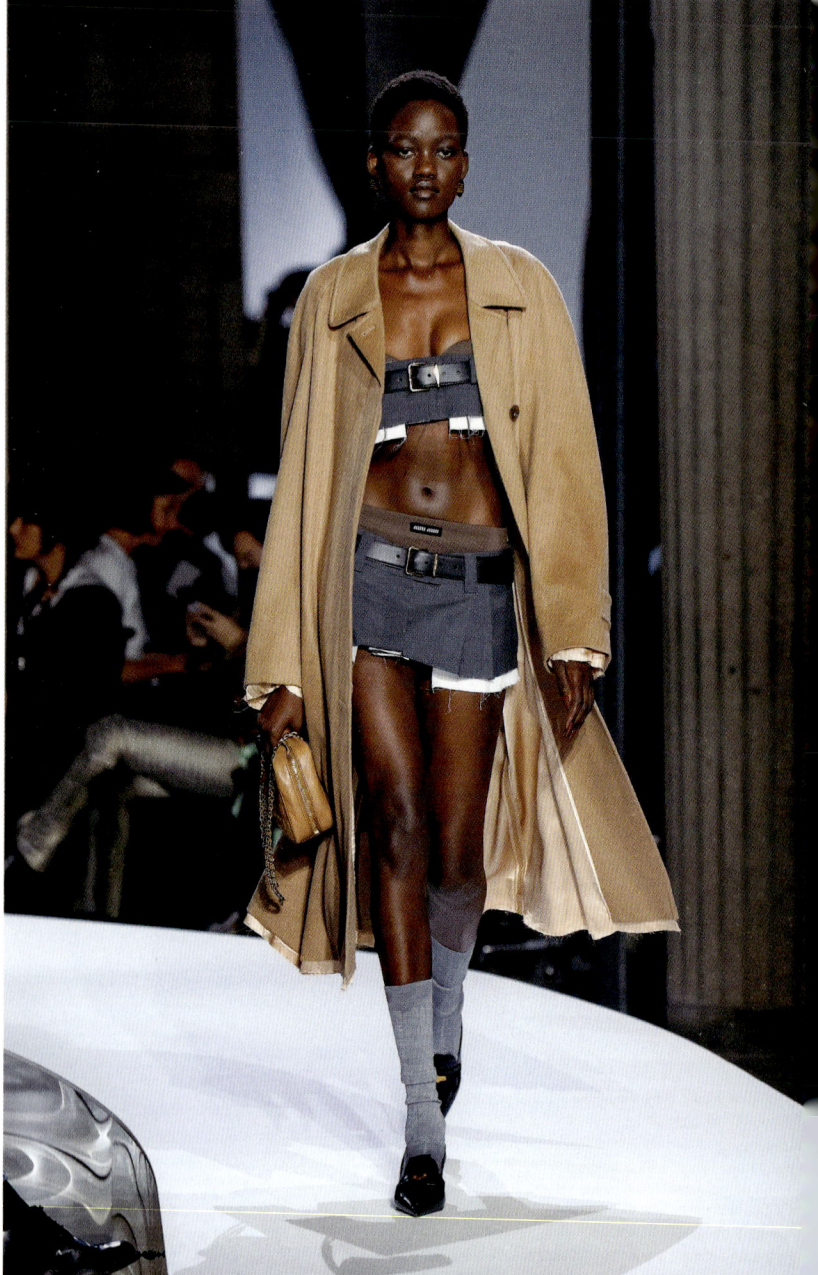

The Viral Micro Mini

When Miu Miu showed its Autumn/Winter 2022 collection at Paris Fashion Week, the internet was ablaze with a sea of reposts about one singular item: a khaki, low-rise micro miniskirt that was so small, it barely covered anything. Styled with a study leather belt and white pockets jutting out from the hemline, it screamed early 2000s culture.

Backstage, after the show, Miuccia Prada told the press, "It's so normal, but for me it's so strange. Strange is not strange anymore." Rarely in fashion in this day and age do things have the ability to shock, and yet, the Miu Miu micro miniskirt did. Granted, the miniskirt has a history of shock value dating all the way back to 1966, when Mary Quant debuted her fashion-history-altering garment called the miniskirt.

Still, there's one major difference between the first and last generations of the miniskirts coming down the runways. While the past conveyed sex appeal and femininity, the minis shown on the Spring/Summer 2022 runway are about owning one's power in a different way. Miu Miu, for example, presented boyish silhouettes, blurring the lines of gender with khaki skirts and navy sweaters, akin to a new kind of uniform; there were hints of intellectualism. The runway show also featured trans models, which created ample discourse online. Worn with chunky socks, penny loafers, ripped-up sweaters and librarian-like baggy button-down skirts, Miuccia Prada once again blurred the lines between sex appeal and Fashion with a capital F.

Elsewhere on the runway, models wore long maxi skirts with little else than a bra and necklace, once again subverting the codes of dressing. The Miu Miu micro mini is about dressing for oneself, rather than putting on a skirt to satisfy the male gaze.

OPPOSITE The Miu Miu micro mini of 2022 shook up the world. It was the most talked about runway moment of the year.

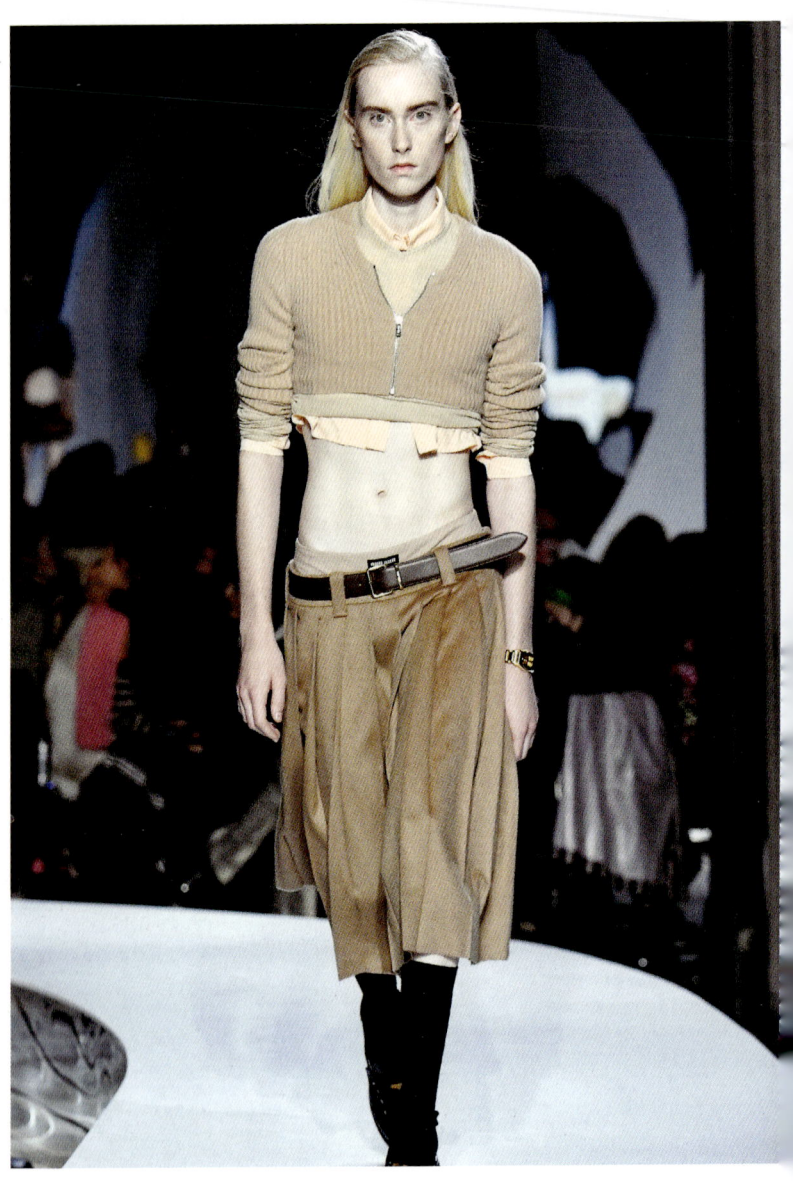

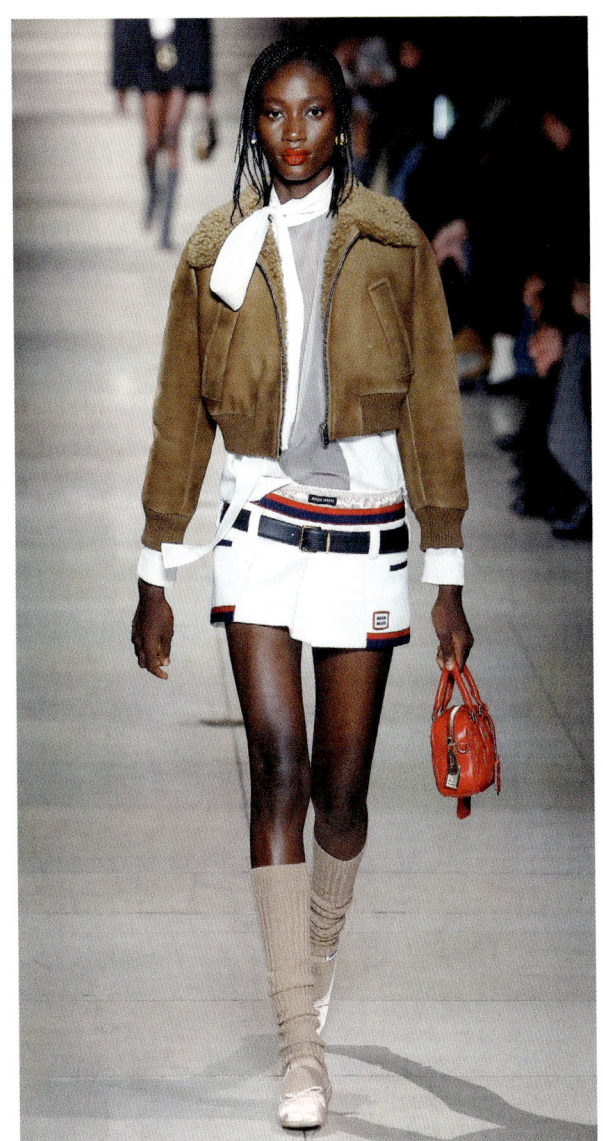

RIGHT Miu Miu maximalized its viral micro mini moment and released many different versions of the style, referencing tennis skirts and school uniforms.

OPPOSITE The brand continues to lean into uniform dressing, borrowing elements like pleated schoolgirl skirts, seen here.

The Bags

While Miu Miu's ready-to-wear and shoes tell so many stories, it's impossible to ignore the fact that the brand has had an iconic history when it comes to bags. For many fans of the brand, the bags were an easy entry point because they were less conceptual and simply more wearable. Much like Prada, the quality was unparalleled. But with Miu Miu, there is still always a gentle hint of unconventionalism.

Miu Miu bags experienced an increase in popularity in the mid 2000s, when celebrities like Jessica Alba, Blake Lively, Rachel Bilson, Rihanna, Zoe Saldaña, Sienna Miller and January Jones wore them. Many of the Miu Miu bags of the past were made of leather with a subversive twist. The Vitello Lux Bow bag was a sizable leather bag with two gorgeous leather bows on either side. The Coffer Hobo, popular in 2011, came oversized with a massive gold buckle. In 2012, Rihanna carried the Matelassé Clutch. The Matelassé technique which creates the effect of quilting without padding is something Miu Miu has used time and time again on bags and in shoes throughout the years. It adds an extra layer of personality and girlishness, just like Miu Miu's ruffles or smocking on a dress. The Miu Miu celeb circle also loved its various editions of the Madras bag, which was typically shaped like a traditional camera bag with a large gold closure in the front.

When Miu Miu was in its maximalist era in the mid 2010s, the bags on the runway strongly reflected that aesthetic. Of course, simplified versions were ready to buy in retail stores across the globe, but Miu Miu held nothing

OPPOSITE Miu Miu bags are some of the bestsellers from the brand and combine its signature wit and practicality.

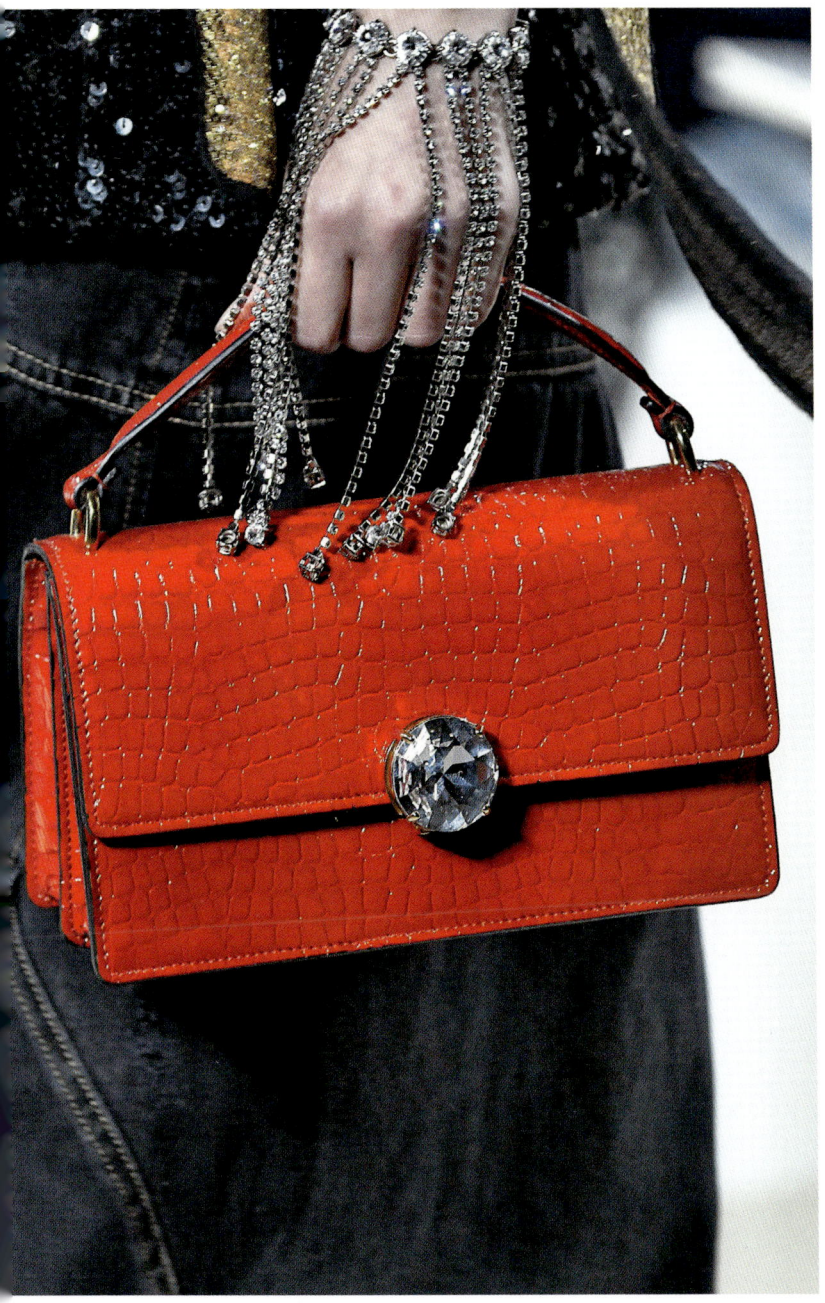

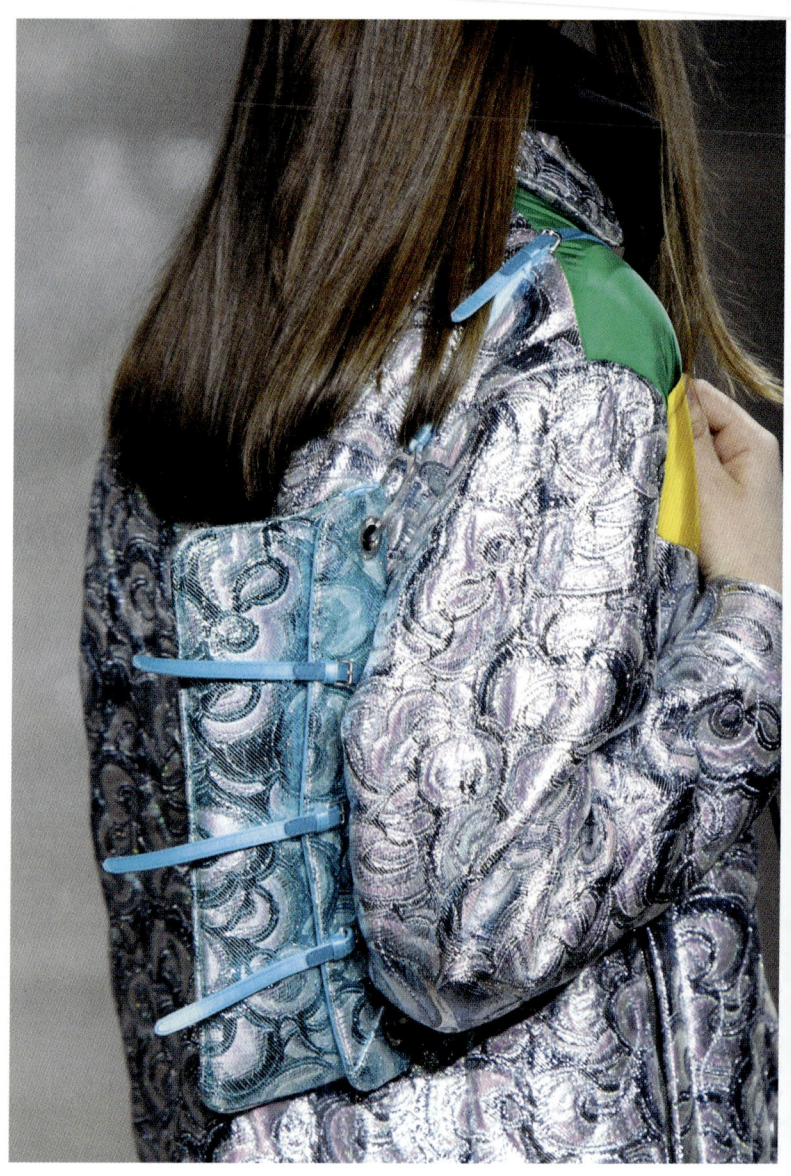

back during these years. For Spring/Summer 2017, huge top handle bags had geometric prints all over them for a totally '70s style. The Autumn/Winter 2015 collection was full of candy-coloured top handle Matelassé bags that had contrasting patches of patent leather. The straps were made of snakeskin with a chunky resin chain link. Sky-blue lambskin trims mixed with leopard print pony hair. Vivid orange python bags came on chunky chains. Bowler bags were decked out in blue, red and grey all at once.

With the increase of social media influencers and celebrity partnerships, Miu Miu's bags have only become more and more popular over the years. And what they may lack in colour and excess, they make up for in genius styling on the runway. Miu Miu has shown bags exploding with shoes and shirts as well as ladylike top-handle bags carried leisurely and strategically in the crooks of models' elbows. Recent must-haves include the Wander bag, which is a crescent half-moon zippered bag done in Matelassé. *Euphoria*'s Sydney Sweeney was the face of the bag's campaign and it's also a favourite of Emma Corrin, Gigi Hadid and Hailey Bieber. Another popular favourite launched in 2023 is the Arcadie, a slim little rectangular top handle bag that comes in traditional smooth leather and Matelassé. The campaign for the bag starred Zaya Wade, Amelia Gray Hamlin, Mia Goth and Ethel Cain and It girls like Alexa Chung and Emily Ratajkowski are fans.

Miu Miu continues to experiment with its bag line, offering a utilitarian approach with a quirk. The brand has created bags with excessively big leather cargo pockets, as well as woven cotton and wicker styles with the logo splashed across them.

OPPOSITE For Autumn/Winter 2014, glittering fabric bags matched the whimsical coats and dresses in the collection.

The Eyeglasses

Miu Miu has always had a strong connection to eyewear. In 2005, Luxottica and Miu Miu signed a worldwide licensing agreement for the production and distribution of Miu Miu frames and sunglasses. Over the years, Miu Miu sunglasses have appeared in different iterations on the runway and in retailers. Most well-known perhaps were the glittery frames and gold metallic cat eye options from the early 2000s, which are still very popular and affordable on the secondhand market today.

But perhaps what no one could have predicted was the rise of Miu Miu's eyeglasses. For the Autumn/Winter 2023 show, many of the models wore librarian chic eyeglasses with frizzy, frazzled hair and sheer slip skirts, oversized fluffy coats and normcore-like layers. With any other runway show, it wouldn't have been anything to take notice of, but with Miu Miu, it created a whole other layer of storytelling and ushered in the brand's new era of geek chic – plus, a celebration of glasses, which is rarely seen in the world of fashion.

The Spring/Summer 2024 collection focused on bringing back the mall culture style of the mid 2010s, from layered polo tops to board shorts, and models here also wore plenty of glasses, adding a major contrast to the look. Even if glasses weren't seen in the subsequent collection, Autumn/Winter 2024 was all about quirky ladylike style with a sense of maximalism and almost every single model wore a pair of dark, blackout sunglasses. To put it simply, eyewear is everything in the world of Miu Miu.

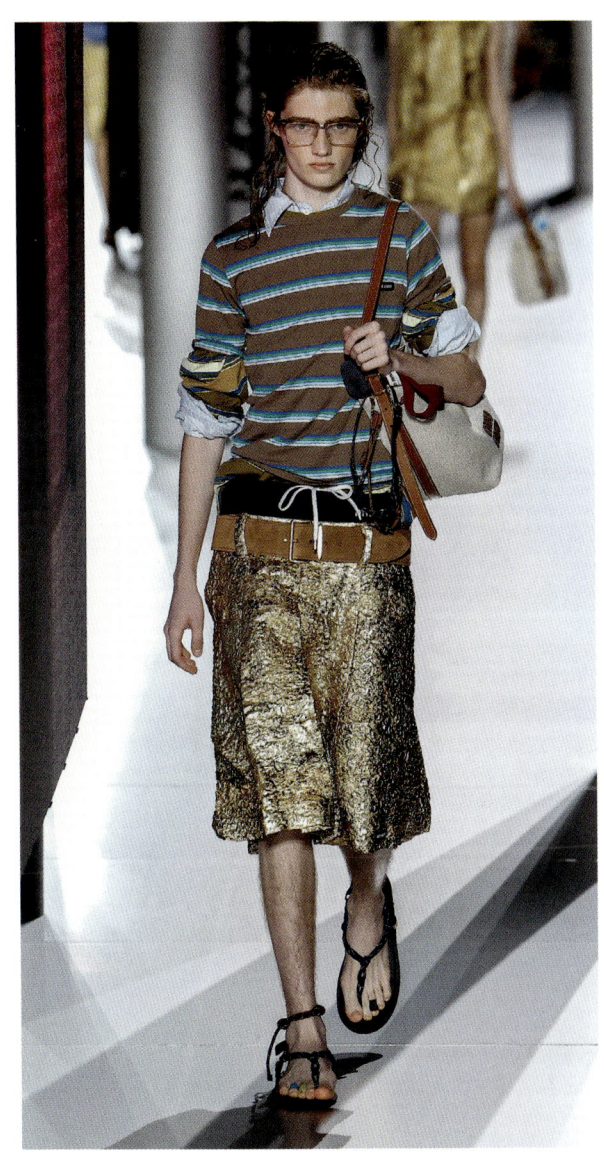

RIGHT Miu Miu has always given eyeglasses a platform and made them a staple of fashion.

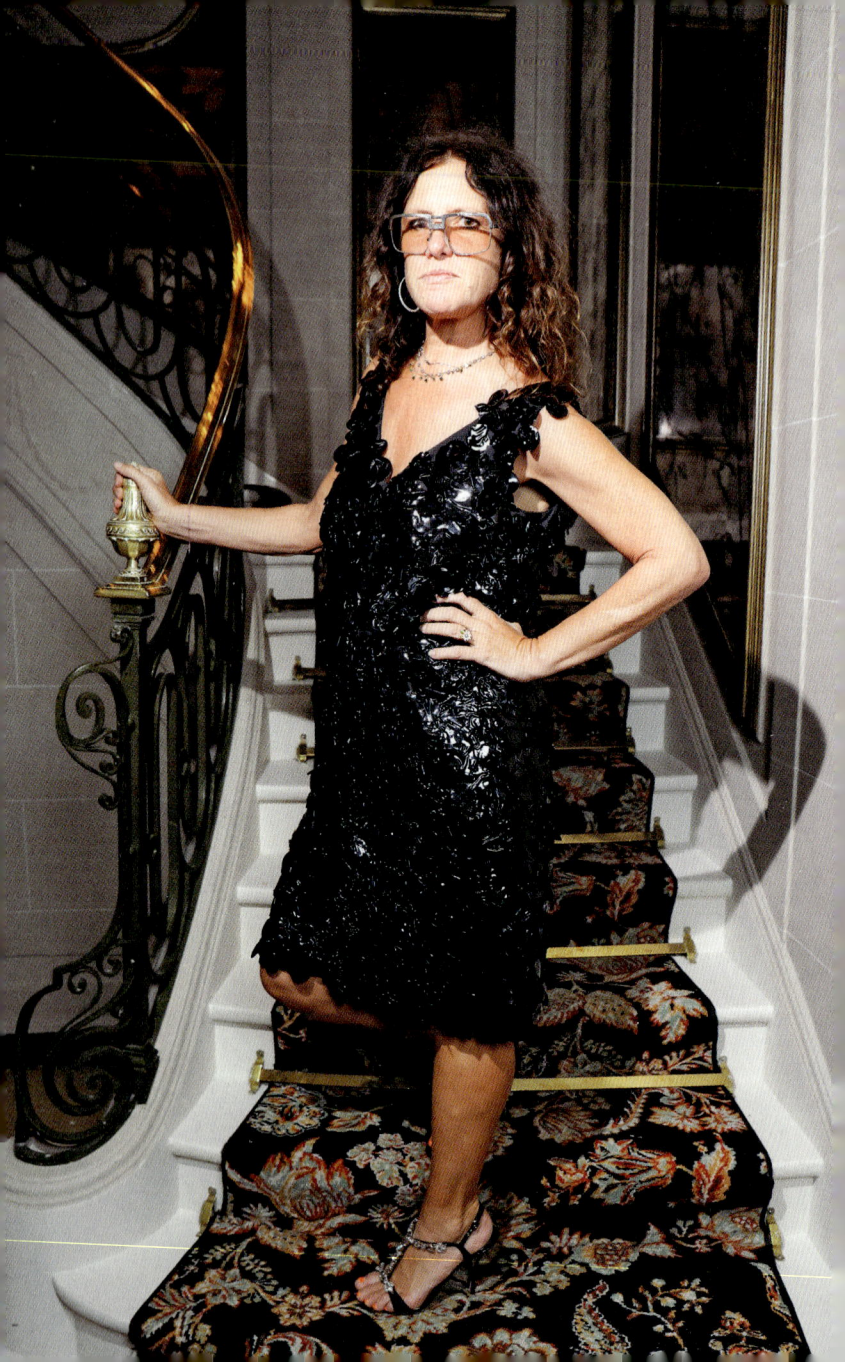

The Katie Grand Years

Likewise, the stylists who have worked with Miu Miu in the capacity of runway shows have had a very distinct point of view which has influenced the way the brand is perceived and conceptualized. For years, the fashion editor and stylist Katie Grand worked with Miu Miu. She first started styling the shows in 2002 and remembers Miuccia Prada herself making bold outfit choices – such as brightly coloured underwear that showed through her white dresses.

An avid fan of Miu Miu and Prada, she often dresses in archival pieces from the brand, mixing and matching pink shearling sandals covered in pearls with cascading sequin dresses and geek chic glasses – the ultimate oddball combinations that Miu Miu was well-known for in the mid 2010s when Grand was styling the shows. She herself reportedly owns over 1,000 pairs of Prada shoes and perhaps her obsessive love of the brand is what made her vision so strong when she did style the shows. "We tend to like the same pieces, and there's definitely a mutual influence in what we wear," she wrote in *System* magazine in 2016. "When I go to see her I'll turn up in Prada, and sometimes Miuccia will ring the store to try on the same piece herself. It works the other way round, too: I'm often inspired to buy something she's wearing."

"In the end, a Prada dress doesn't wear you, you wear the dress, even if it is covered in bottle tops and you leave sequins all over the place when you dance," Grand told the *Guardian* in 2013.

OPPOSITE Creative director Katie Grand's work and style is instantly recognizable for being dramatic, larger than life and maximalist.

The Lotta Volkova Years

In 2020, Lotta Volkova, a Russian stylist, began working with Miu Miu, styling the looks in a way that took inspiration from zany real-world situations punctuated with irony. Think: the tops of underwear showing, handbags overstuffed with high-heeled shoes and clothes, or even the layering of big puffy gloves with ladylike peacoats and pearls.

Volkova formerly worked very closely with Balenciaga and Vetements under the Demna era, transforming these brands and helping them to acquire cult-like status early on. Before that, she had her own clothing brand. She herself dresses in odd combinations, using shock value to combine streetwear culture with high fashion and a big dose of irony. "I'm interested in looking at things differently. I'm interested in looking at something that we aren't necessarily used to being considered beautiful," she told *Vogue* in 2016. "I'm interested in showing another side of things which I do find beautiful, which I do find real and interesting. I'm not necessarily interested in bad taste or kitsch, either –it is just something that I look at differently. I'm interested in showing another side of things. Don't get me wrong, I like beautiful things too, but going beyond the classic boundaries of beauty seems much more interesting to me. I like digging under appearances, going deep."

She has a knack for creating a certain buzz that has mass cool appeal. And it is under her styling direction that the brand had many, many viral moments. "She's always looking for something that's unseen," Volkova told *T* magazine of working with Miuccia Prada.

OPPOSITE Lotta Volkova has a knack for creating timely styling moments that seem to go viral.

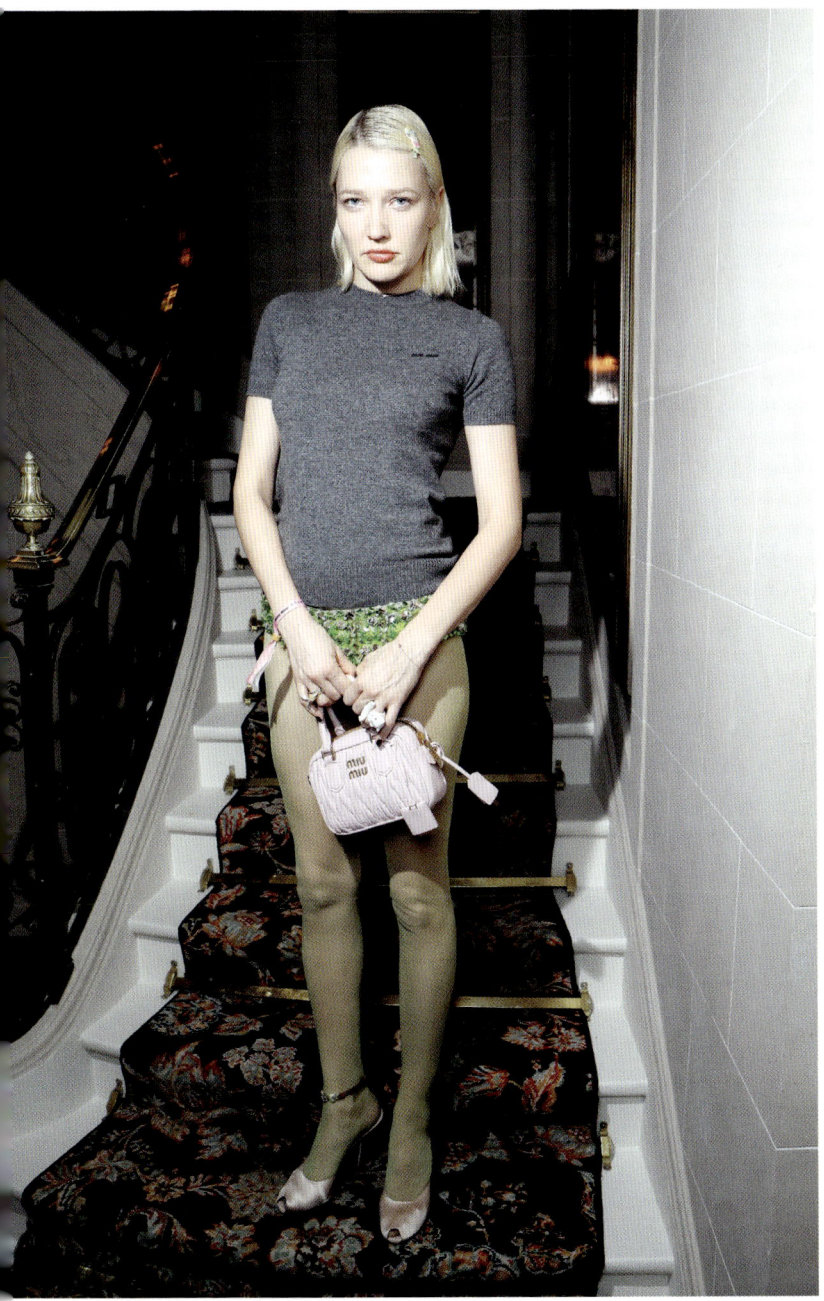

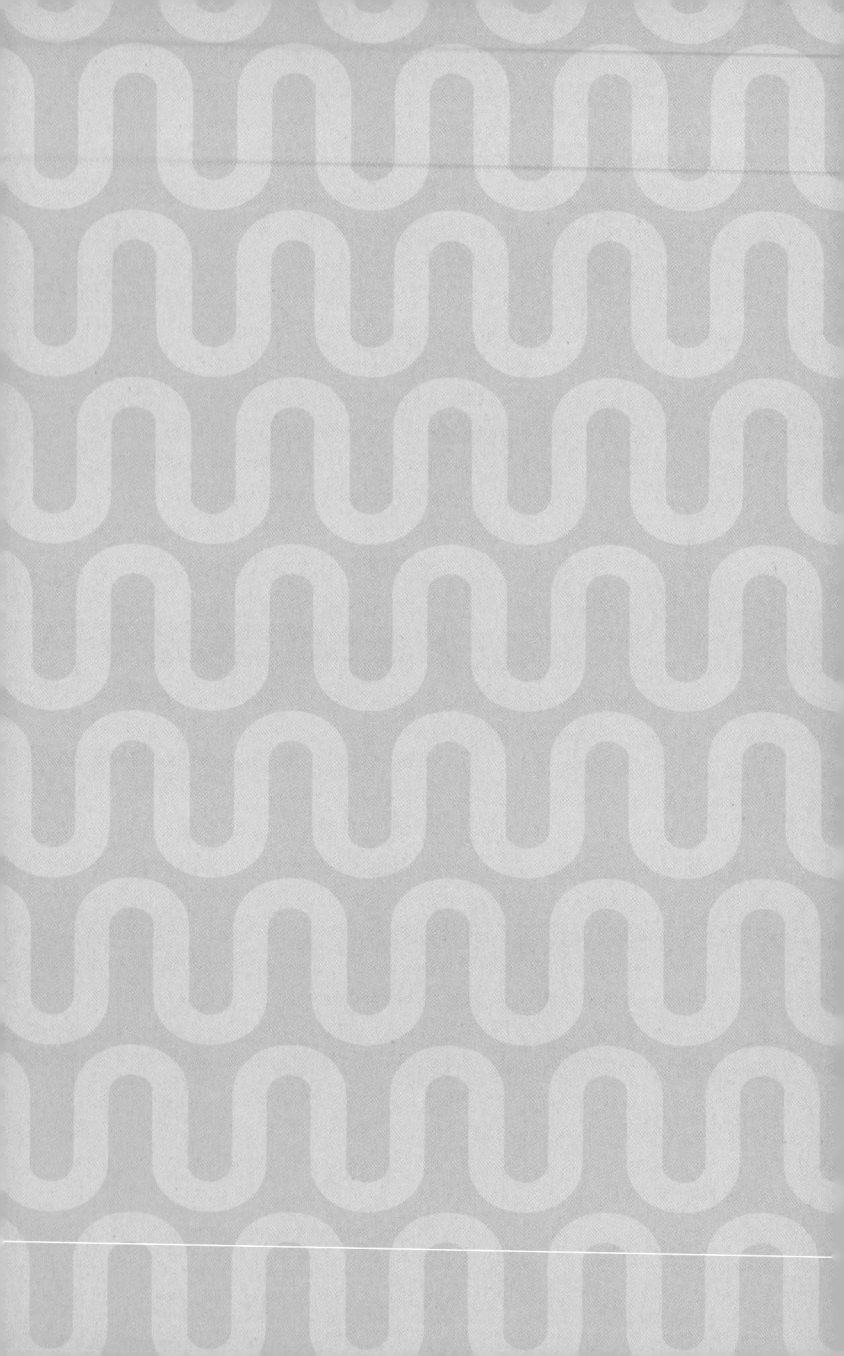

miu miu
muses

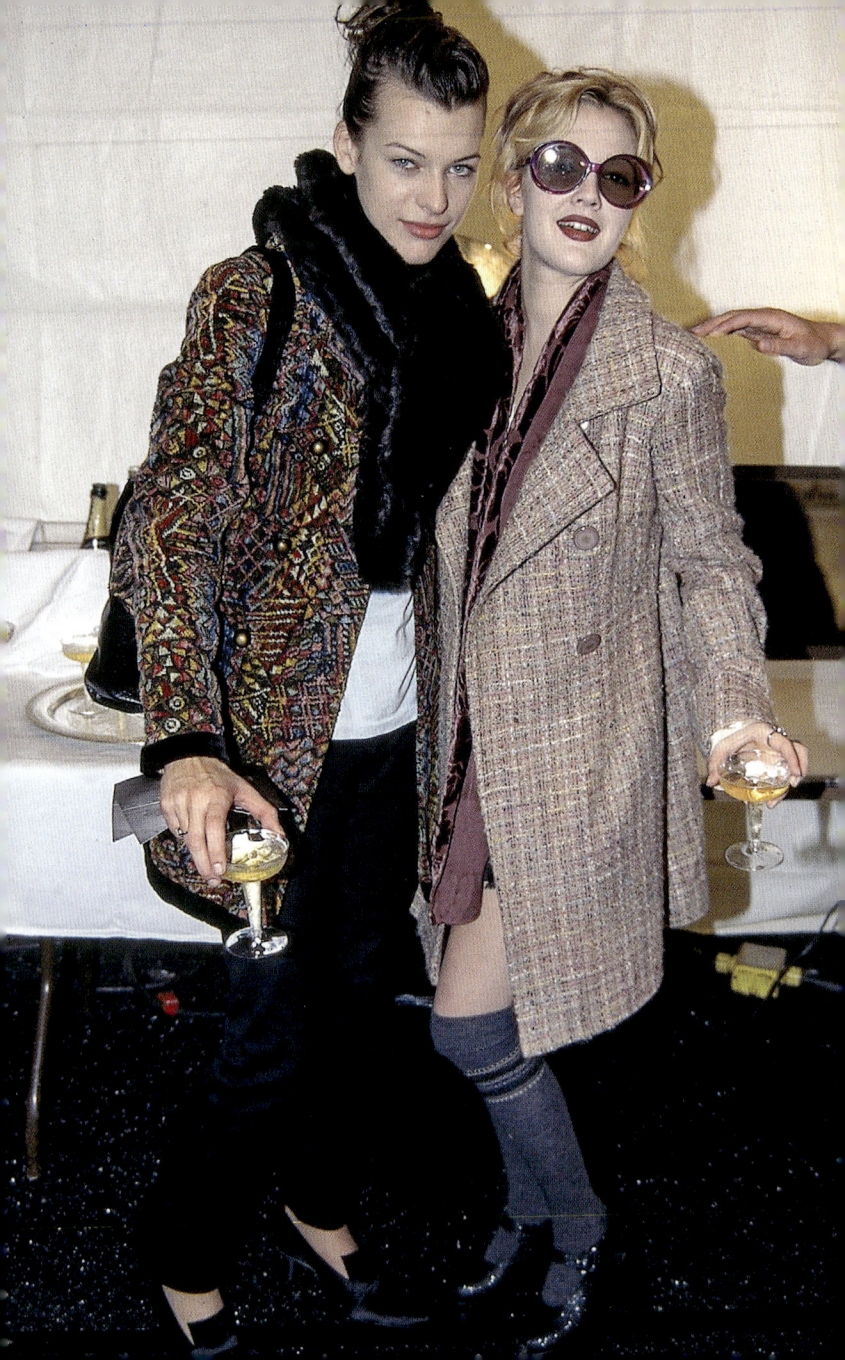

miu miu
'it' girls

Miu Miu has never shied away from having an interesting casting that goes far beyond the traditional idea of the model. In the world of Miu Miu, these people subvert the idea of the muse and become a building block of the brand.

Early on, Miu Miu cemented itself as a brand that was at the forefront of celebrities as muses. For the Spring/Summer 1995 campaign, Miu Miu cast Drew Barrymore as the star, photographed by Ellen von Unwerth and styled by Joe McKenna. Against a series of glowy, pastel backdrops she posed with her hair and make-up done like a 1920s silent film star: skinny brows, dark lips and rosy blush. Dressed in little button-downs, silky midi skirts and heeled Mary Janes, she represented Miu Miu's affinity for girlish cool with a rebel streak. The starlet was also the main event of the Autumn/Winter 1996 campaign. Styled with punky, spiky hair and dark black eyeshadow, she wore the pink peacoats and brown, librarian-like wool skirts with a very specific energy. Barrymore was the first celebrity ambassador for the brand. In fact, there are muses who have been a part of the pack since the very beginning. Like Chloë Sevigny, who opened the Spring/Summer 1996 runway show while wearing a simple periwinkle

OPPOSITE Actresses Milla Jovovich and Drew Barrymore backstage at a Miu Miu show in New York in 1995.

polo and matching pants. It was one of Miu Miu's most important shows, since it was one of the very first and took place in New York. Sevigny is a fashion icon today, but back then she was very early on in her career. It was two years after the *New Yorker's* legendary profile of her in 1994, and it was hot off the heels of her starring in the film that made her ubiquitous: Larry Clark's *Kids*. Like Barrymore, she later starred in the Miu Miu campaign for 1996.

RIGHT Model and actress Adwoa Aboah is one of the icons in Miu Miu's circle of muses.

OPPOSITE Actress Chloë Sevigny has worked with Miu Miu since its early days and opened the Spring/Summer 1996 show.

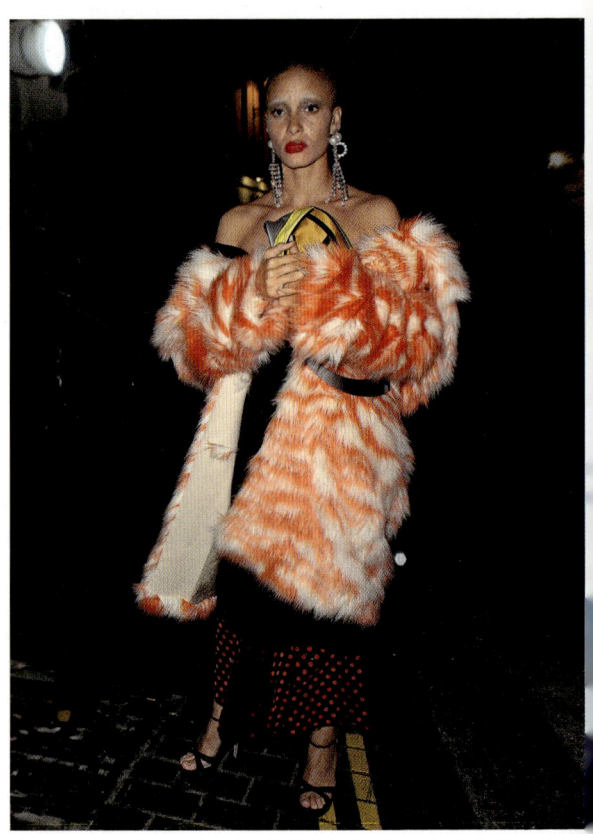

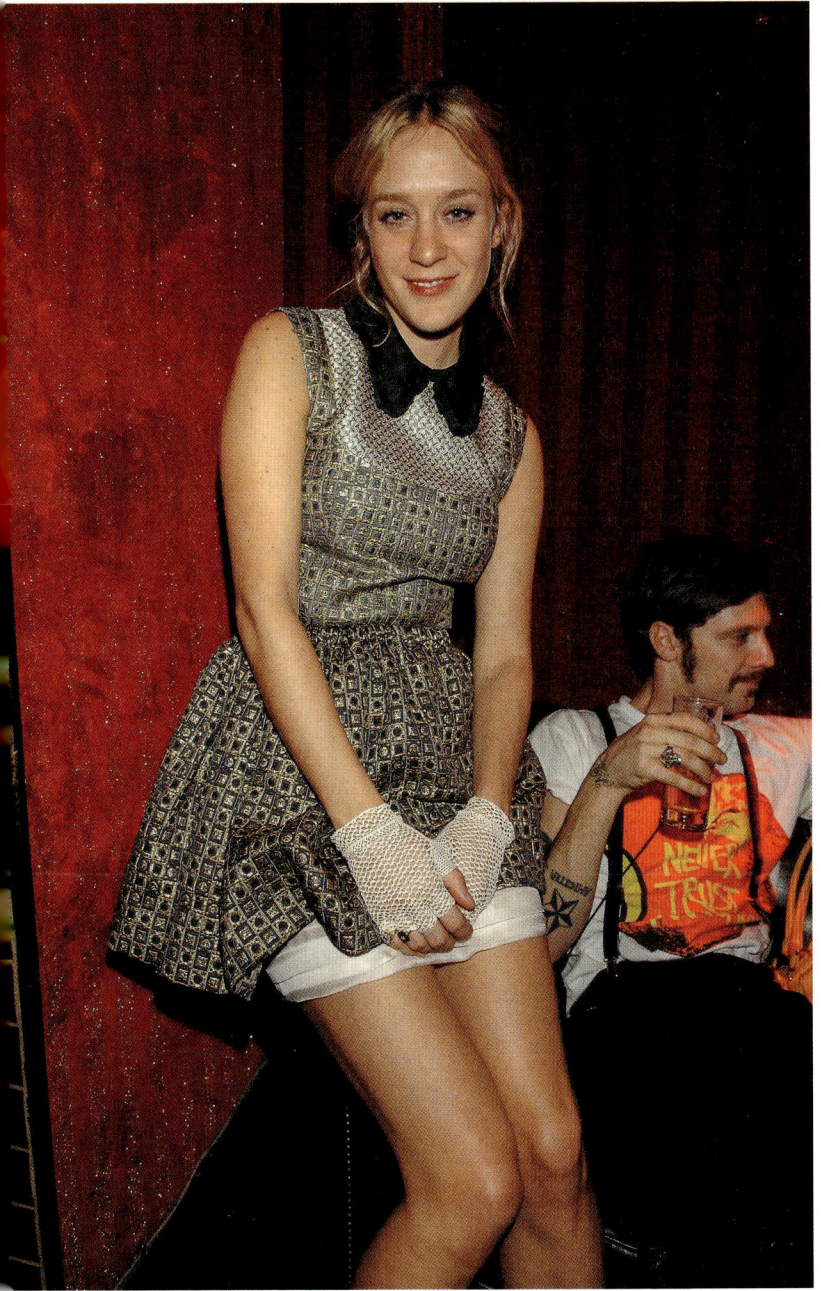

It's been decades, and Sevigny is still collaborating as a muse. In 2017, she took over as the director for the Miu Miu *Women's Tales* and created *Carmen,* which follows the comedian Carmen Lynch and was shot on 35mm film in Portland, Oregon. "It might sound corny, but I love the Miu Miu girl," she told *Vogue* at the time. "I love the perverted fantasy of it. I love the brand, so it's easy for me to get behind it and be excited to be working with them. Because I love the clothes, I love the shows, I love the ads

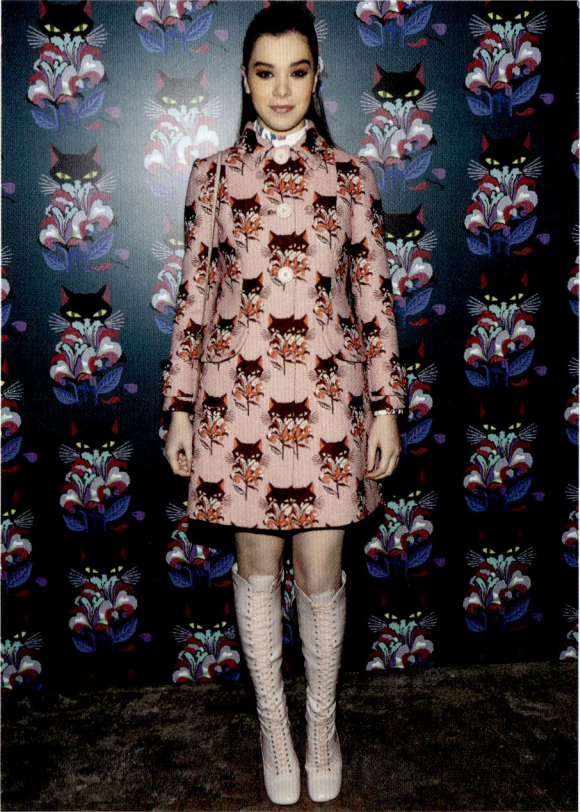

LEFT Actress-singer Hailee Steinfeld wearing one of the legendary Miu Miu cat coats.

OPPOSITE Miu Miu muse Chloë Sevigny walked in the brand's debut runway show in New York City.

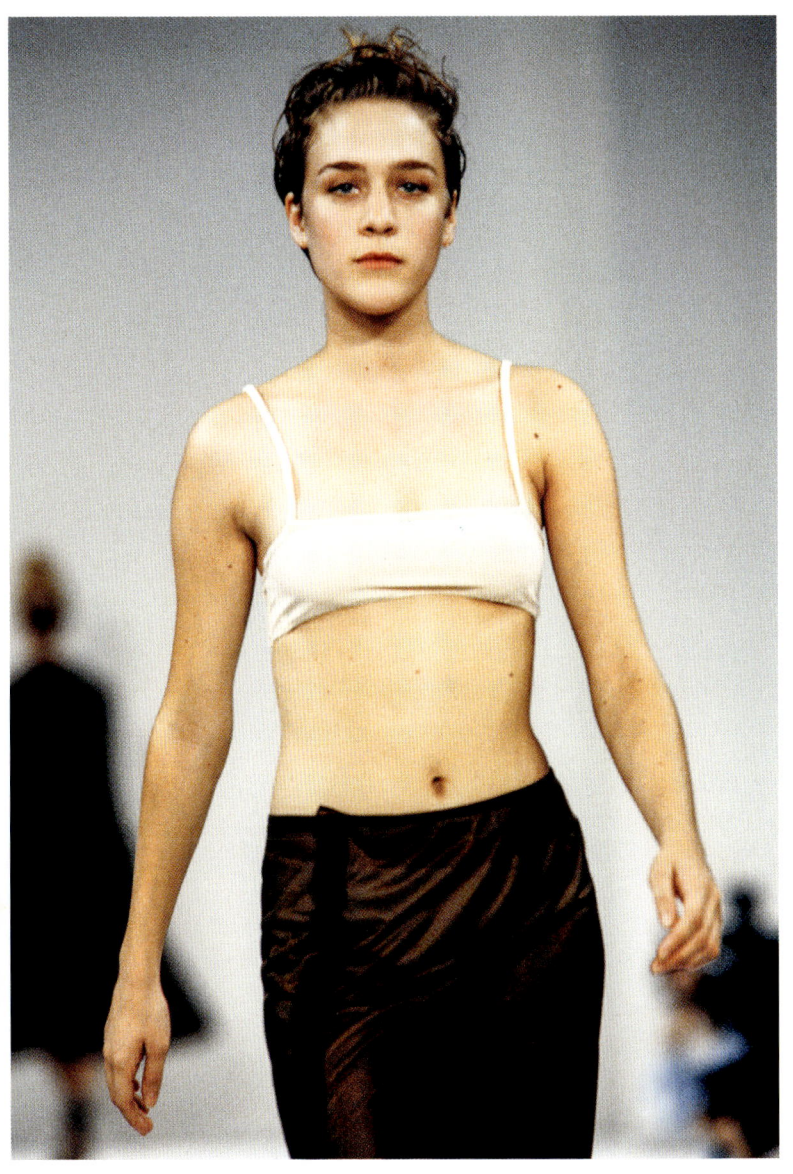

and the way she celebrates actresses, especially actresses that are in controversial works because I'm so attuned to that." Miu Miu has often been cited as a brand that feels very much ahead of the trends, and working with Sevigny early on only proved that they were quick to recognize a kindred spirit.

Miu Miu campaigns have served as a sort of rite of passage for It girls around the world throughout time. For Spring/Summer 2008, Kirsten Dunst was the face of the brand. Photographed by Mert & Marcus, art directed by Ezra Petronio and styled by Joe McKenna, she is pictured against surreal red velvet and navy-blue backdrops behind a theatre curtain. It's fitting for a collection that took inspiration from Pierrot, Harlequin, French maids and *Swan Lake*. The brand described the campaign as "An utterly absurd combination of elements interlace with one another, blurring the line between on-stage and backstage, public and private, fantasy and reality, performance and intimacy. These dichotomies highlight the multiplicity at the core of Miu Miu."

The campaigns have been lensed by some of the most talented photographers in the world, from Corinne Day to Ellen von Unwerth and Glen Luchford. Likewise, they often feature celebrities as stars. For Autumn/Winter 2005, for example, Selma Blair was the campaign star alongside Lou Doillon, Evan Rachel Wood and Eleanor Friedberger, photographed by Inez & Vinoodh. Photographed on a grey quilted velvet sofa, they are shown mid conversation, mid pose or applying one another's make-up. They wear black lace dresses with visible underwear showing, suede skirts embellished with flowers and tartan coats with fuzzy fur collars.

OPPOSITE Actor Emma Corrin fast became a Miu Miu favourite for their experimental sense of dressing.

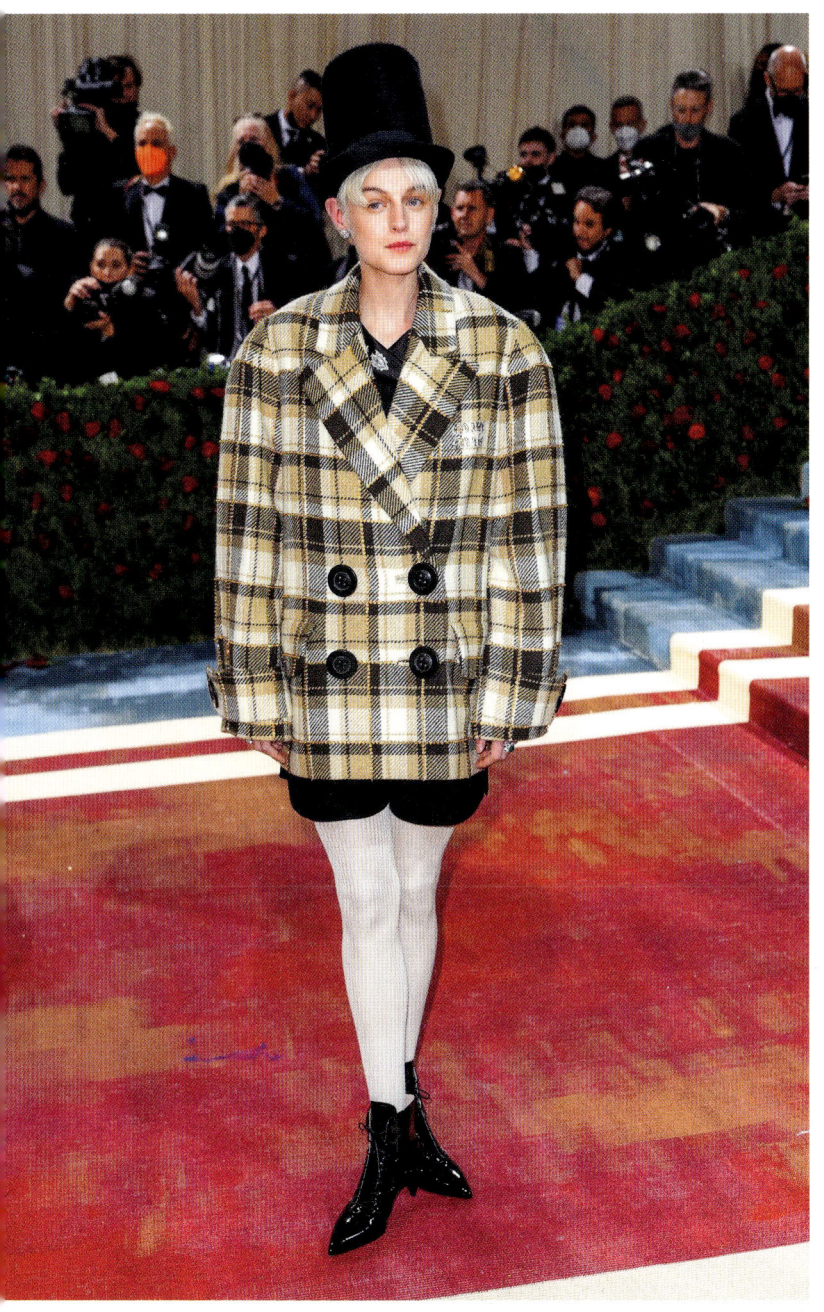

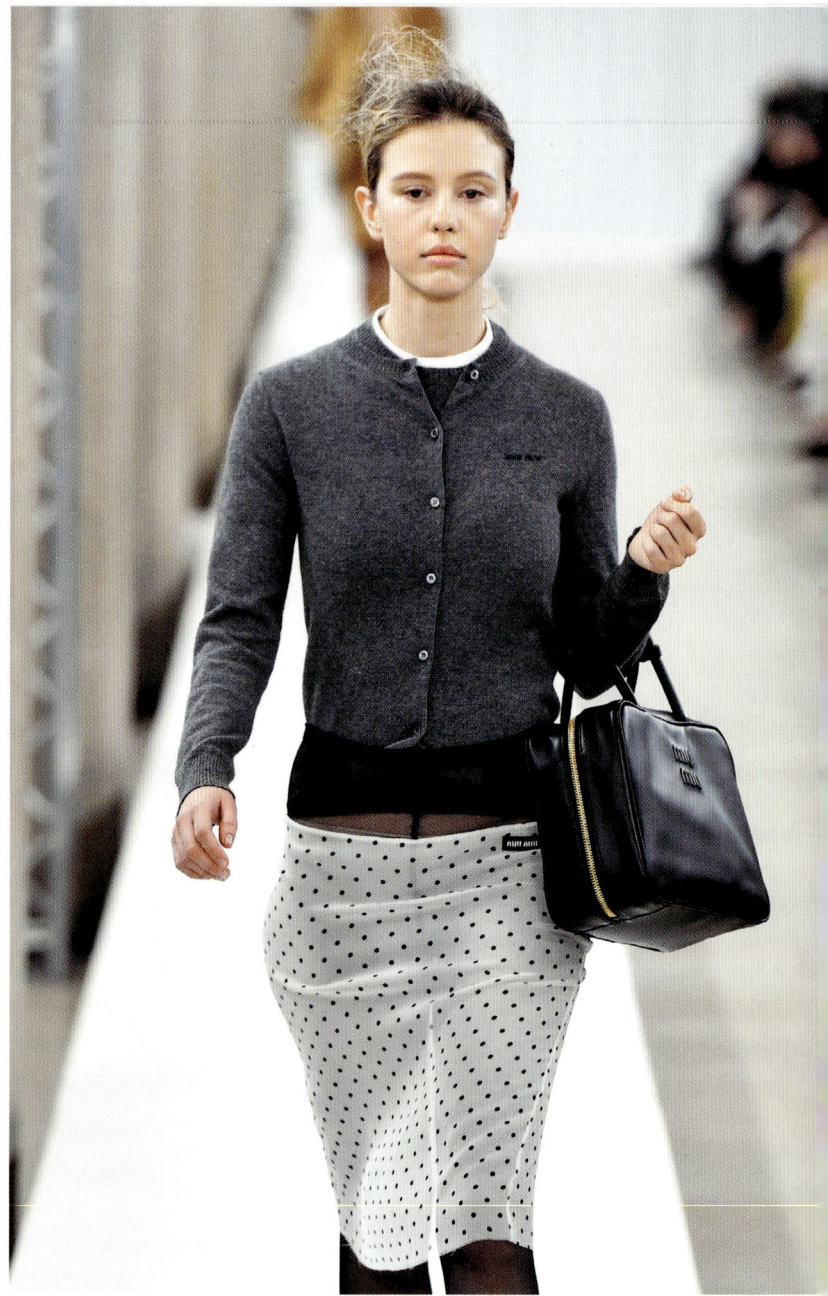

For Miu Miu's Spring/Summer 2006 collection, Kim Basinger and Camilla Belle were the campaign stars of choice. They lay together on a crushed velvet bedspread, posing in star-printed gowns, white eyelet shirts, and shirts with big cargo pockets, their heels on and their bags planted firmly in sight. In one image, Basinger stares back at herself in the bedroom mirror. In another, she wears white chunky sunglasses indoors, despite the dim lighting. The campaign was once again shot by Inez & Vinoodh.

Miu Miu campaigns have a way of creating an uncomfortable energy that speaks volumes about being a woman and being perceived as a woman. This time, the brand explained the shoot with, "The process is about capturing an intimate moment of creative energy, where we stand witness to the complex relationship between past, future, and contemporary interpretations of femininity and beauty."

For Spring/Summer 2015, Steven Meisel photographed Marine Vacth, Mia Goth and Imogen Poots all in interior settings through a slightly ajar door. In fur-trimmed coats, glossy leather jackets and with their bags on their laps, they alternate between making eye contact and looking off into the distance, a visual commentary on perception between public and private spaces. To further hit the nail on the head, some of the models wore the signature glitter frame glasses to shield themselves. Goth, who was 22 at the time, was positioned on a bed with white sheets. In the UK, the Advertising Standards Authority (ASA) banned the ad for "sexualizing a model who appears to be underage". According to Miu Miu, it was all about the idea that "these cinematic tableaux are filled with a sense of tension, an entwined narrative on the edge of dénouement, as we view these women's stories and the collection through a series of captivating, interrupted moments."

OPPOSITE Actress Mia Goth has starred in Miu Miu campaigns and walked the runway for the brand.

Muses on the Runway

After decades of featuring mostly traditional models on the runway, Miu Miu started swapping a few conventional models for familiar faces. Take, for instance, Resort 2019, when the brand showed inside the Hôtel Regina in Paris. Guests crowded around the decorative lobby in seats that were staged to form a mock runway. There were collegiate-style sweaters with a crystal embellished, Miu Miu twist, '60s-inspired gowns and bags covered in cat prints, and acid-washed denim minidresses trimmed with bright plumes of ostrich feathers. But perhaps the biggest surprise? The casting. The actress Rowan Blanchard opened the show in a stunning draped navy-blue maxi dress, featuring a strap covered in leopard print, crystals and feathers. *Stranger Things*' Sadie Sink, Chloë Sevigny and Gwendoline Christie also walked the runway and to the surprise of almost everyone in the room, Uma Thurman closed the show.

For Autumn/Winter 2020, Storm Reid, the then 16-year-old actor of *Euphoria* fame, opened the show in a glowing copper gown. The singer Rita Ora also walked the runway. Today, it's become somewhat expected to see celebrities and a unique batch of characters on the Miu Miu runway. These choices not only serve as the conventional muse relationship, but also embody the mood and feeling of the collection at the time of being presented. For the Spring/Summer 2023 collection, a slew of people who embodied the Miu Miu muse walked in the show, including the musician Ethel Cain, the director Miranda July, the It girl and model Emily Ratajkowski and the singer and songwriter FKA twigs. For Autumn/Winter 2023, Miu Miu had Emma Corrin, Amelia Grey Hamlin and Mia Goth walk in the show. Also, Miu Miu continued experimenting with gender fluidity, casting gender-fluid models as well as male models to wear some of the newly re-introduced menswear.

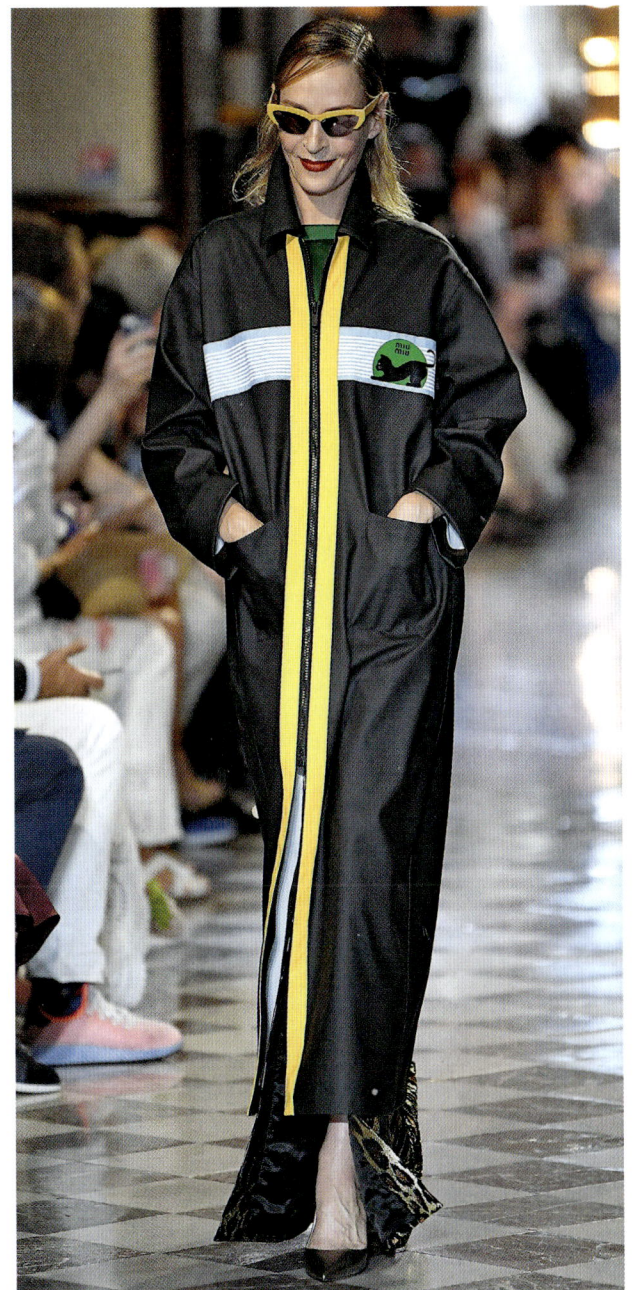

RIGHT Uma Thurman surprised the audience when she walked in Miu Miu's Resort 2019 show.

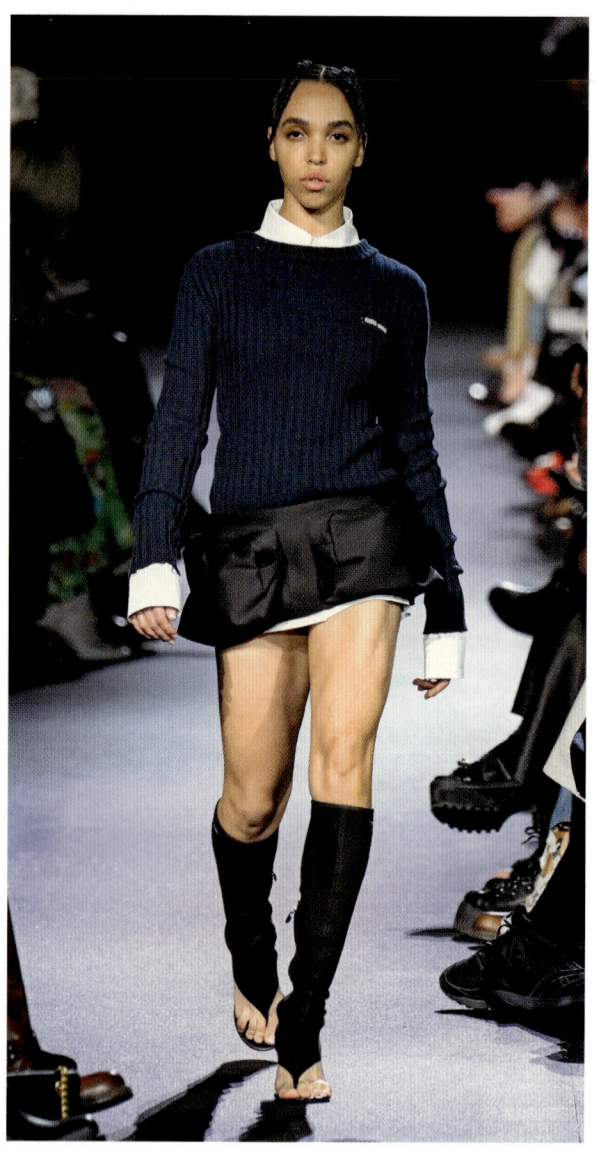

LEFT Miu Miu's runway castings are always interesting, mixing personalities and celebrities like singer-songwriter FKA twigs, seen here.

OPPOSITE Singer-songwriter and actress Rita Ora also walked the Miu Miu runway.

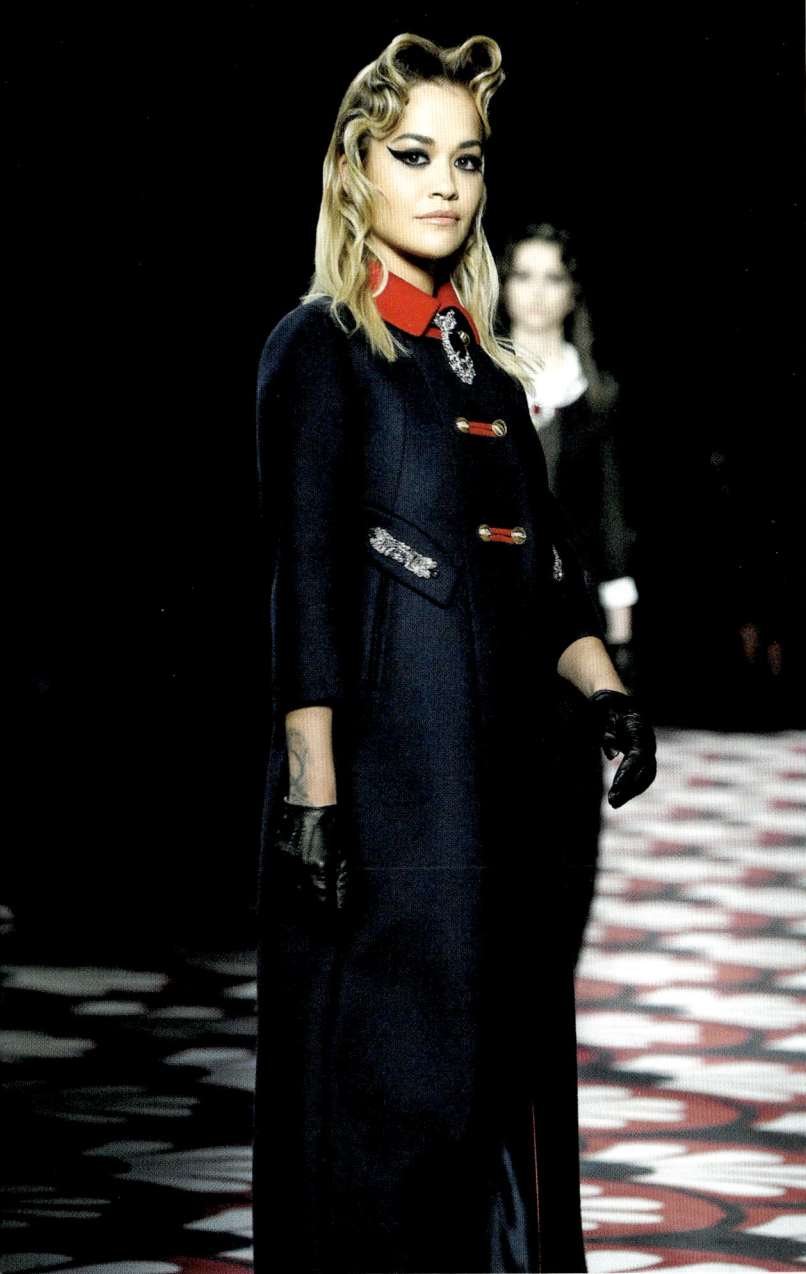

But it was perhaps the Autumn/Winter 2024 show that created the biggest statement. Among all the regular Miu Miu models was not just a celeb but a superfan of the brand and an unconventional muse. The Guangxi-born, 70-year-old Dr Qin Huilan, who has amassed a huge collection of archive Miu Miu and Prada, was asked by the brand to walk in the runway

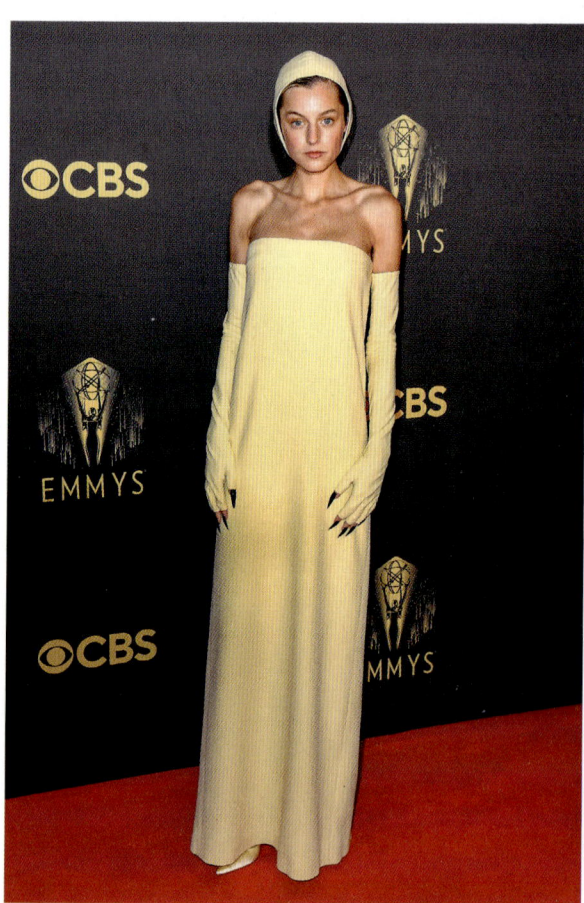

RIGHT Another iconic Miu Miu look worn by Emma Corrin.

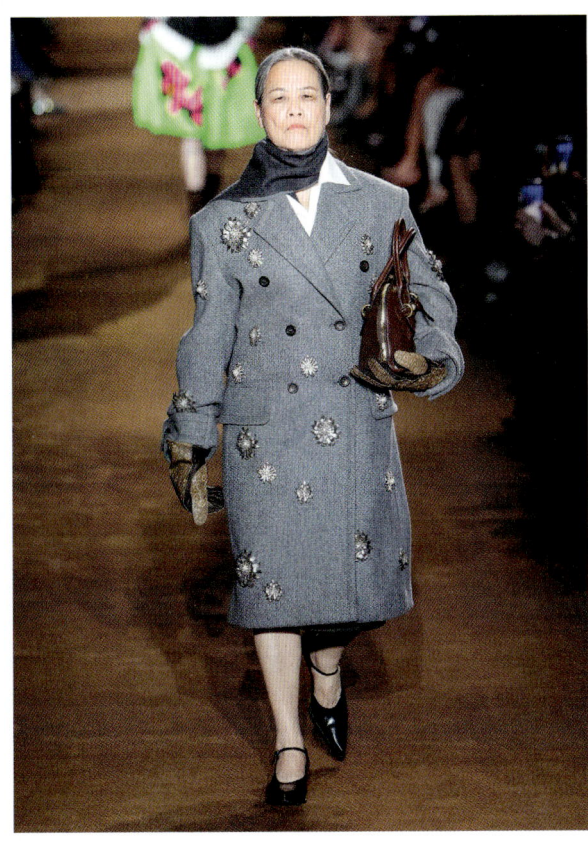

LEFT Dr Qin Huilan, a superfan of the brand and then 70 years old, walked the runway for Autumn/ Winter 2024.

show. The retired doctor started an Instagram account in 2022, inspired by her son, and Miu Miu reached out after seeing her many outfits on the platform. For the runway show, she wore a long grey peacoat covered in silver flower embellishment with a scarf, oversized gloves and a brown leather handbag. As for shoes, she donned a pair of black pointed-toe Mary Janes. The actress Kristin Scott Thomas also walked in the show, as did Ethel Cain, Angel Haze, Little Simz and Jasmin Savoy Brown.

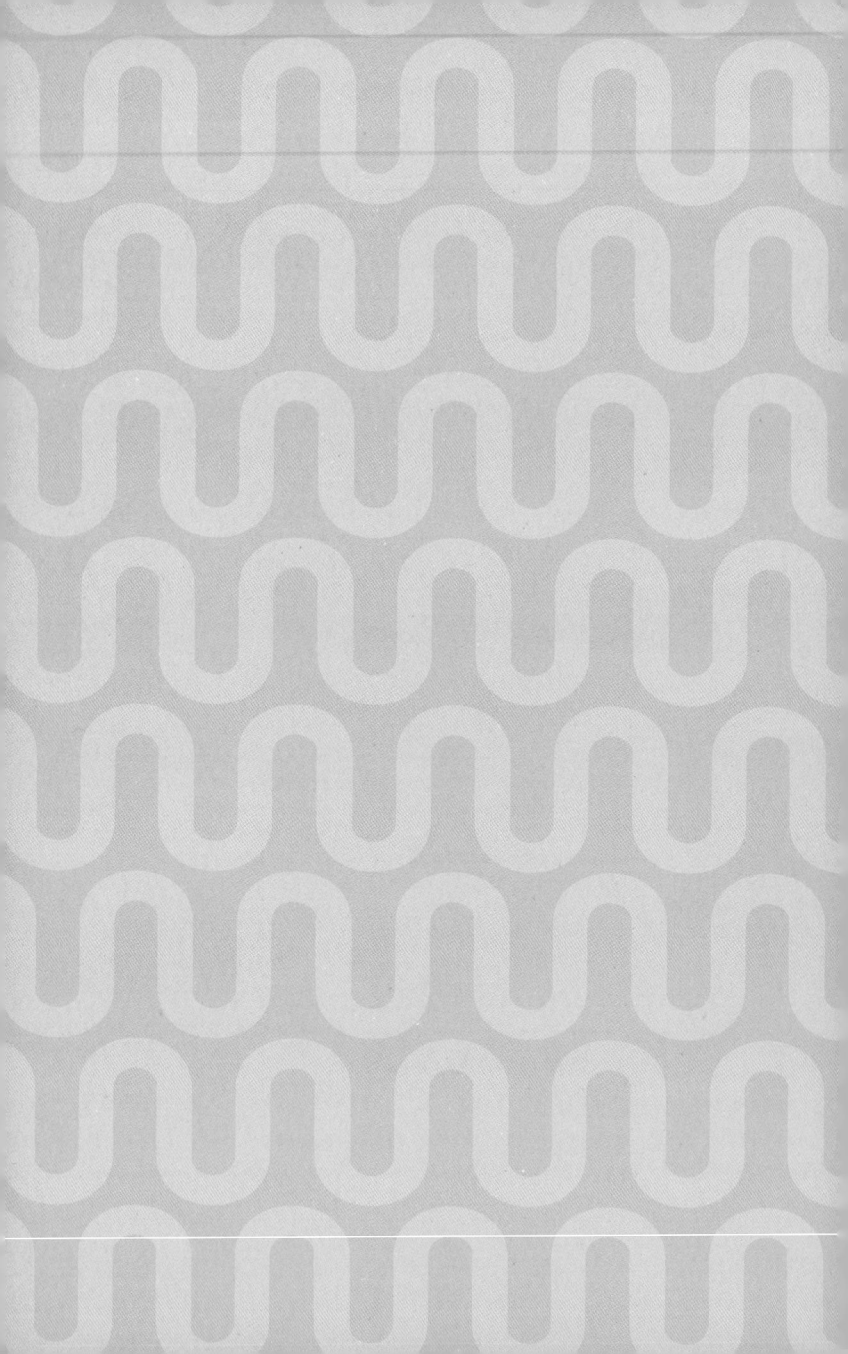

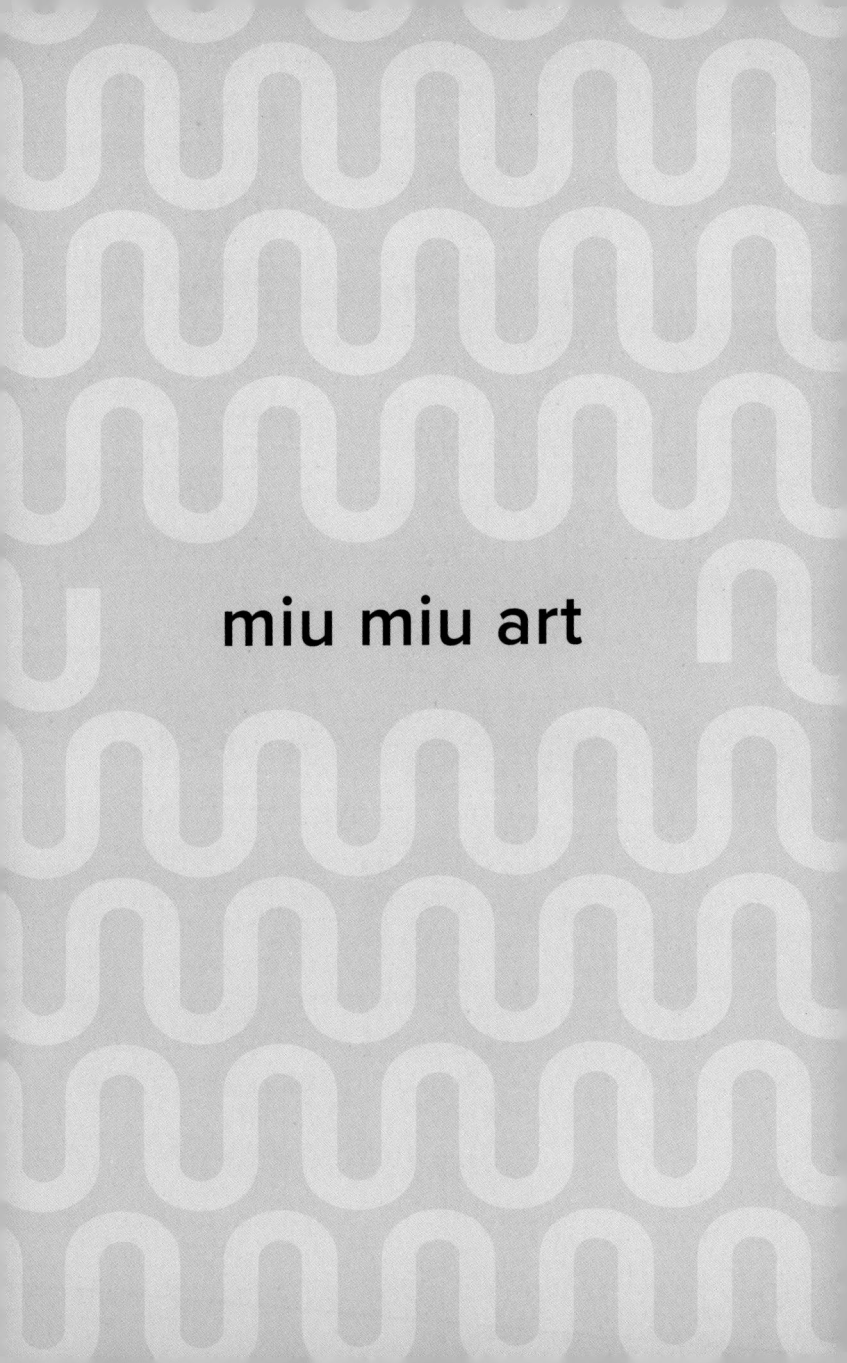

miu miu art

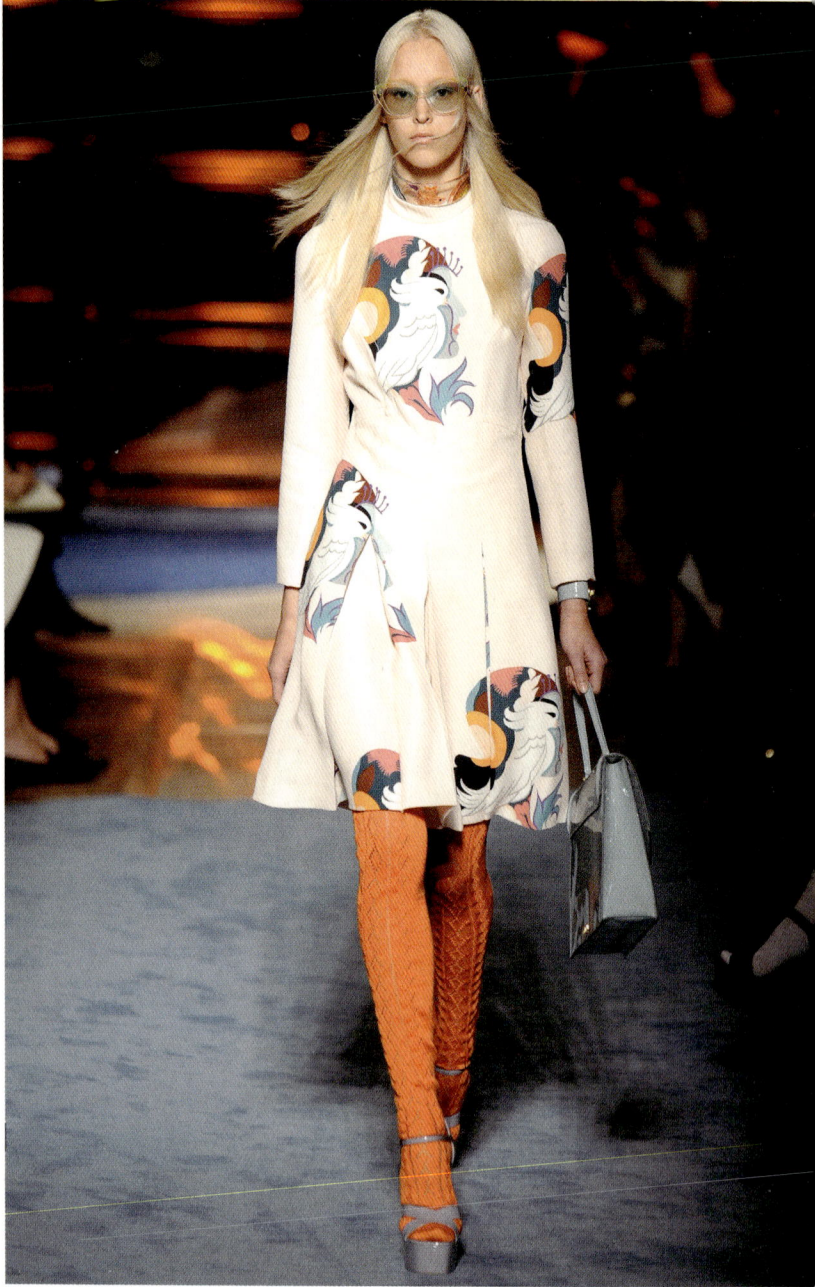

the art of miu miu

Ever the intellectual, Miu Miu embraces art in a myriad of different ways. Take, for example, the fact that the brand has been uplifting female directors through film commissions since 2011. The series, called *Women's Tales*, sees Miu Miu asking female directors to interpret the spirit of the brand.

Miu Miu on Film

Miu Miu's *Women's Tales* are often poetic and experimental, allowing the director to have full rein over the aesthetic impact. The films feature different aspects of the female experience, from marriage to motherhood and beyond, hence the title of the series, *Women's Tales*. Directors have come from all over the world and have included Ava DuVernay, Miranda July, Agnès Varda, Chloë Sevigny and Dakota Fanning. These films typically all debut as a world premiere at the Venice Days section of the Venice International Film Festival and are often also celebrated by the brand with parties around the world.

OPPOSITE One of the Miu Miu artist collaborations, this time with illustrator Jeanne Detallante.

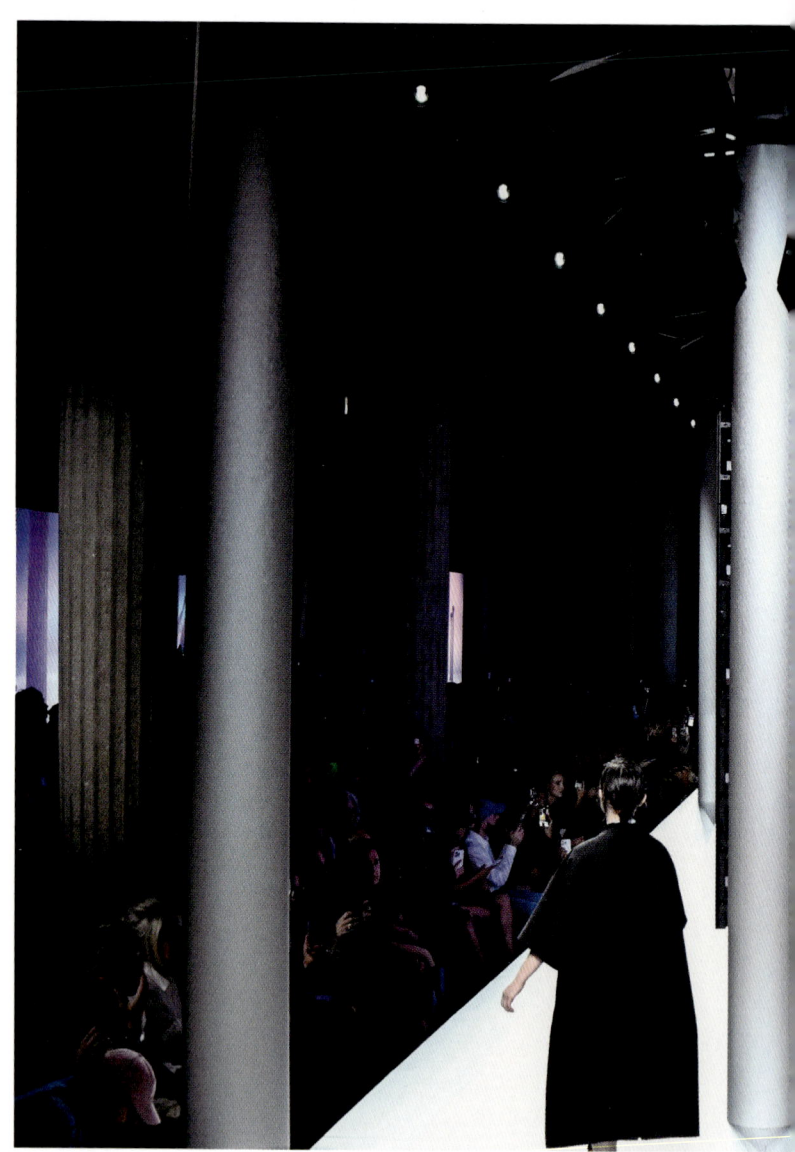

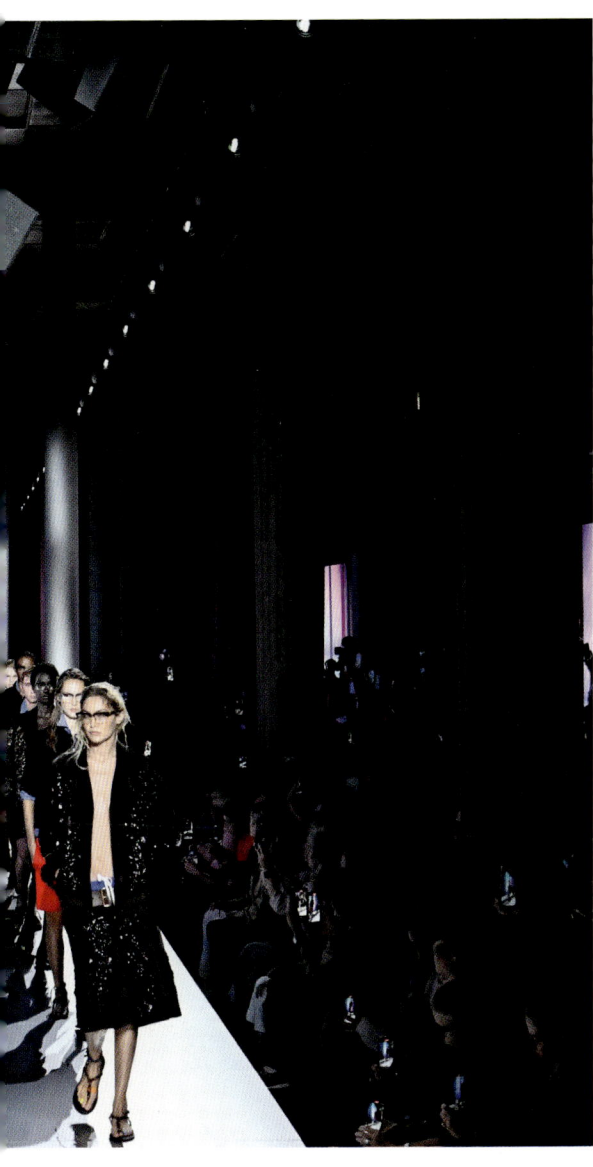

LEFT For each show, Miu Miu transforms the Palais d'Iéna, architect Auguste Perret's masterpiece, into a different artful installation.

Installations

Beyond film, the brand recently began inviting artists from around the world to collaborate on the Miu Miu runway show by creating immersive video displays to hang over the runway. The show always takes place inside the historic Palais d'Iéna in Paris. With its majestic winding staircases at either end of the interior, art screens hang throughout the venue. "They can do whatever they want, but they comment on my show. It's like adding content and enlarging the discussion," Miuccia Prada told *W*. Artists come from all around the world and have included Meriem Bennani and Shuang Li. As the models march by on the runway, the audience gets to watch the live art installation at play. Typically abstract, each video installation poses discourse and thought starters on current cultural topics – from AI to plastic surgery.

In addition to the immersive video screens that have been present at Miu Miu shows as of late, the venue is typically emblematic of the collection itself. The Palais d'Iéna has been transformed by the Dutch architect Rem Koolhaas and his design studio, OMA, into every different, experimental expression of creativity under the sun. It has been covered in curly purple faux fur or floor-to-ceiling posters. There have been benches put together like riser bleachers. For the Spring/ Summer 2022 show, guests each had their own brown leather Eames chair to sit on, as the paper-white runway was raised to snake around the venue in an organic pathway. According to the brand, the collection was an "exercise in referencing and researching reality, using the existing to create the new". The artist Meriem Bennani took over the typical live stream that usually happens during every Miu Miu show and mixed in a series of fantasy sequences starring her mother to blur the lines between real and unreal.

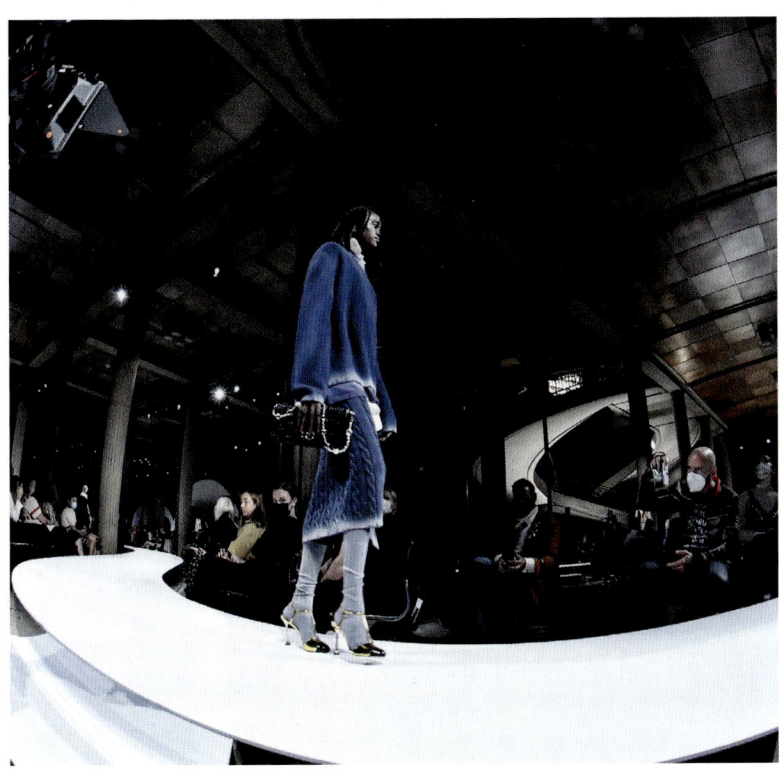

Every season, Miuccia Prada reportedly gives Koolhaas free rein of the set for both Miu Miu and Prada. "We like to keep them completely free," she told *WWD* in 2013. "They come with many ideas and we choose one. It's basically an architectural idea. For a few years, the architectural set was kind of enough. But now, I feel that nothing is never enough, and you have to say more. This is another point that has become very important. That in this vast world, if you want to be heard and you want to be listened to and you want to have a voice that is relevant, you have to not be so subtle. You have to say more."

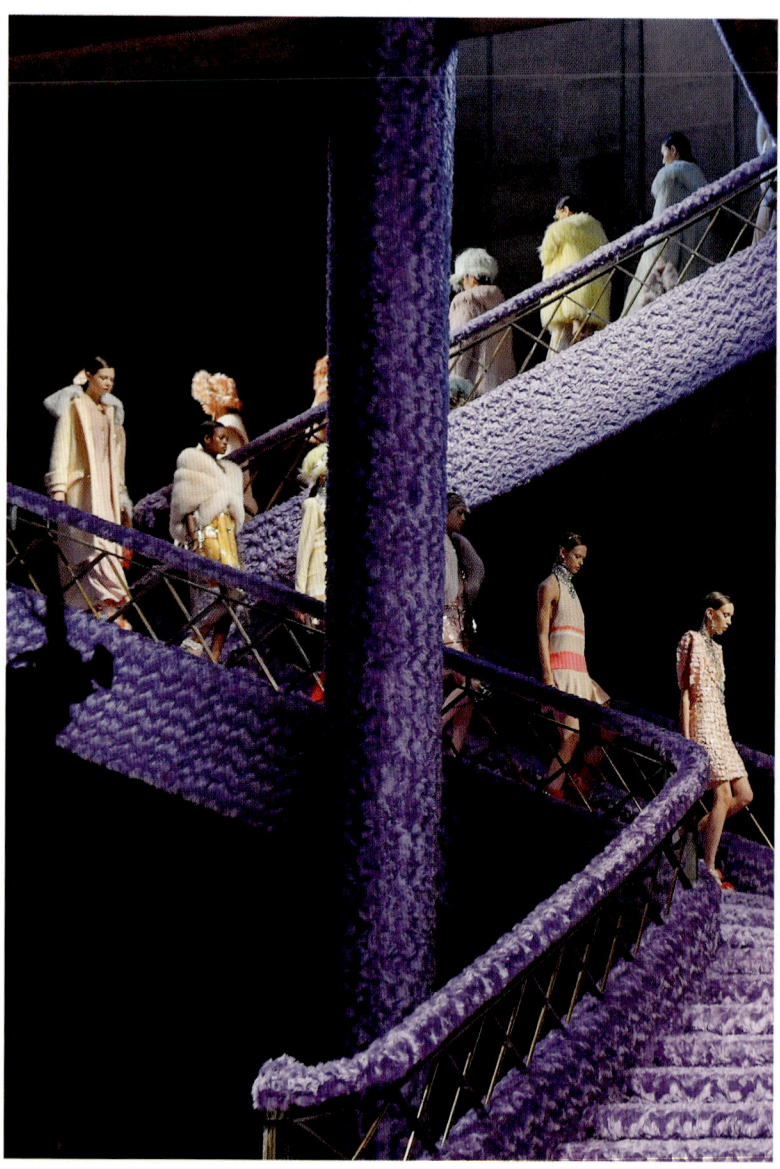

Costumes

As another form of art, Miu Miu has engaged in costume design, but only for very specific projects. Miuccia Prada has collaborated with the director Baz Luhrmann for several films. She worked directly with costume designer Catherine Martin to create looks for *The Great Gatsby* (2013), taking inspiration from the Prada and Miu Miu archives. Miu Miu was a natural choice, with its various vintage inspirations as well as its supple fabrics like chiffon, silk and velvet, often with excessive embellishment that looks straight out of the Jazz Age. Plus, the collaboration was natural since the characters were originally wearing Prada and Miu Miu to get into the mood for all the test shots. "[Miuccia] always sees the future with vintage eyes, and I think Baz kind of always sees the past through modern eyes, so there's an interesting nexus of thought," Martin told *Entertainment Weekly*.

Luhrmann and Martin are frequent collaborators with Miu Miu. The relationship first began via Prada, with *Romeo + Juliet* (1996); the designer created a suit worn by Leonardo DiCaprio. Luhrmann later created a series of short films for the Met's 2012 Costume Institute exhibition "Schiaparelli and Prada: Impossible Conversations" (2013). The trio teamed up again for *Elvis* (2022), designing custom outfits and revisiting garments from the two brands' archives. The film starred Austin Butler as Elvis and Olivia DeJonge as Priscilla, and there was quite an emphasis on Priscilla's outfits. Her floral print dresses, ruffled collar dresses and beaded tops are pure Miu Miu.

OPPOSITE For Autumn/Winter 2017, Miu Miu wrapped its usual show venue in curly purple faux fur to match the aesthetic of the collection.

Fondazione Prada

Taking the brand's commitment to art another step further, Fondazione Prada opened in Milan in 2015. Designed by long-standing creative partner Rem Koolhaas and OMA, the location itself is a work of art – gilded buildings are juxtaposed with industrial designs that house the artwork, which ranges from film to painting, sculpture and beyond. The Bar Luce café sits at the heart of it all, with an interior designed by the famed film director Wes Anderson. Here, the Miu Miu take on art and culture is shown to an extreme. The café is also the perfect setting to wear Miu Miu's intrepid prints, off-kilter colours and zany combinations of underwear as outerwear or sheer skirts with baggy polo tops. But if you were ever wondering if Miuccia Prada considers fashion art, you might get your answer here too. Typically, there are no clothes, accessories or bags on display. Only fine art. The closest thing to fashion as art might just be the inclusion of Louise Bourgeois's installation "Cell (Clothes)" (1996). Here, dresses and trousers collide with harsh wooden doors. "I'd decided that I wanted to keep it separate from fashion. And no one knew – I never told anybody," she told *T* magazine.

Without art at Miu Miu, we'd be without some of the greatest prints in the canon of the brand. When firmly in its maximalist era, the brand frequently teamed up with various artists and illustrators to create mind-bending prints. For Spring/Summer 2014, Miu Miu hired Jeanne Detallante, a Parisian illustrator and visual artist, to create the legendary cat coats and '60s-style dresses that were covered in colourful abstract imagery that blended the look of a rainbow face and a bird. Around the same time, Detallante worked with Prada to create the graphic and geometric faces that covered

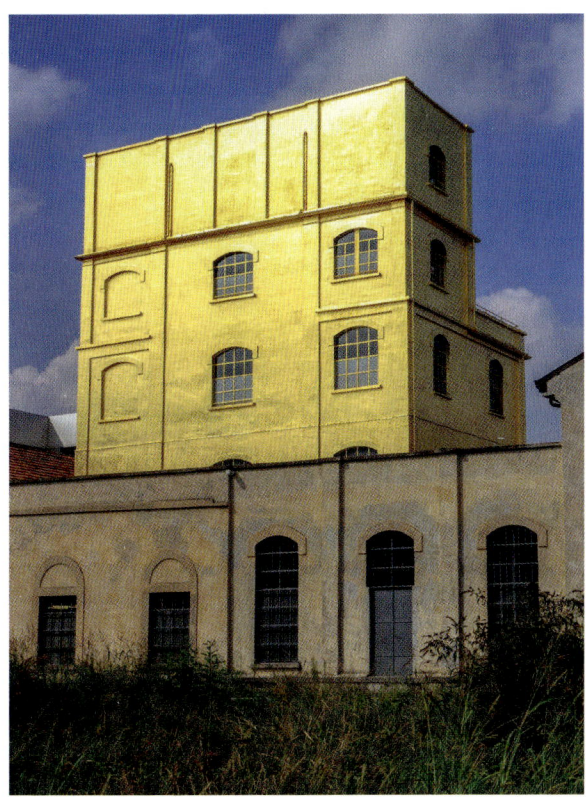

LEFT The enigmatic Haunted House at the Fondazione Prada, which houses ever-changing exhibitions. The building dates back to the early 1900s.

the crystal-studded coats and sporty dresses at Prada. As per usual, Miuccia Prada played with the scale of perceptions of womanhood, touching on the icon of the showgirl as well as the girl, the cat-covered coats representing the scale of a child's coat turned adult. "I asked myself, 'What is classic? Why does it become classic?'" she told *Vogue* backstage after the show. "People think that it is romance, but that's not it – it is something instinctive. Why do women like pink and bows? I am always very intrigued by what attracts people so much."

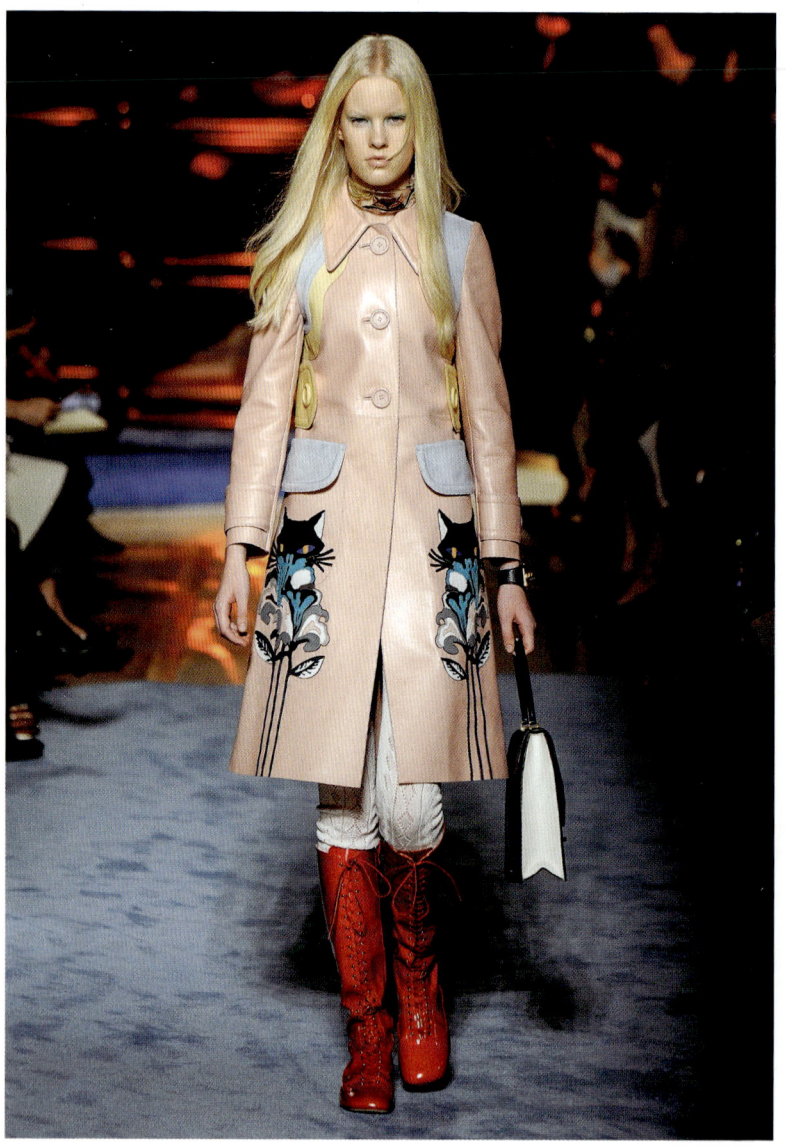

Artist Collabs

In 2015, Miu Miu made another epic art collaboration on the runway, this time with Eri Wakiyama, the New York-based illustrator behind some of the most exciting Miu Miu pieces. Prada's longtime stylist, Olivier Rizzo, introduced the artist and designer, and the rest was history. For Miu Miu's Spring/Summer 2016 runway show, Wakiyama drew lighters dripping with flames and spider-like flower blooms which were placed on gothic fairy Victorian dresses with ruffled collars. The pieces were equal parts nightgown and ballgown and the prints certainly added their own hint of extreme quirk. "Really, Miu Miu was about irrationality," Miuccia Prada said of the collection backstage. "The times we are in are extreme. There's conservatism on both the right and left in politics. And then, people look for escapes from it, attracted to strange religious beliefs or underground clubs and music." The artist would go on to work with the brand on several other collections, drawing designs for everything from T-shirts to long swing coats covered in blooming blossoms and boiler suits. For Miu Miu's Resort 2018 collection, Wakiyama's witchy doll-like girls, scribbled flags and florals had a huge impact, appearing on car mechanic-like work jackets and those same boiler suits.

Yet, even with all the influence of art on Miu Miu, Miuccia Prada maintains a separation between the ideas of art and fashion. She strongly believes that fashion isn't art. "I make a difference, that fashion is not art," she told *Document Journal* in 2015. "It's creative, it's very creative. The only thing it has in common is the creativity. But it is completely different because…well, there's all the polemic that the art world is more commercial! But art is working on absolute ideas, conceptual ideas in general."

OPPOSITE Illustrator Jeanne Detallante has created prints for Miu Miu and Prada, one of her most memorable being the cat print for Miu Miu's Spring/Summer 2014 collection.

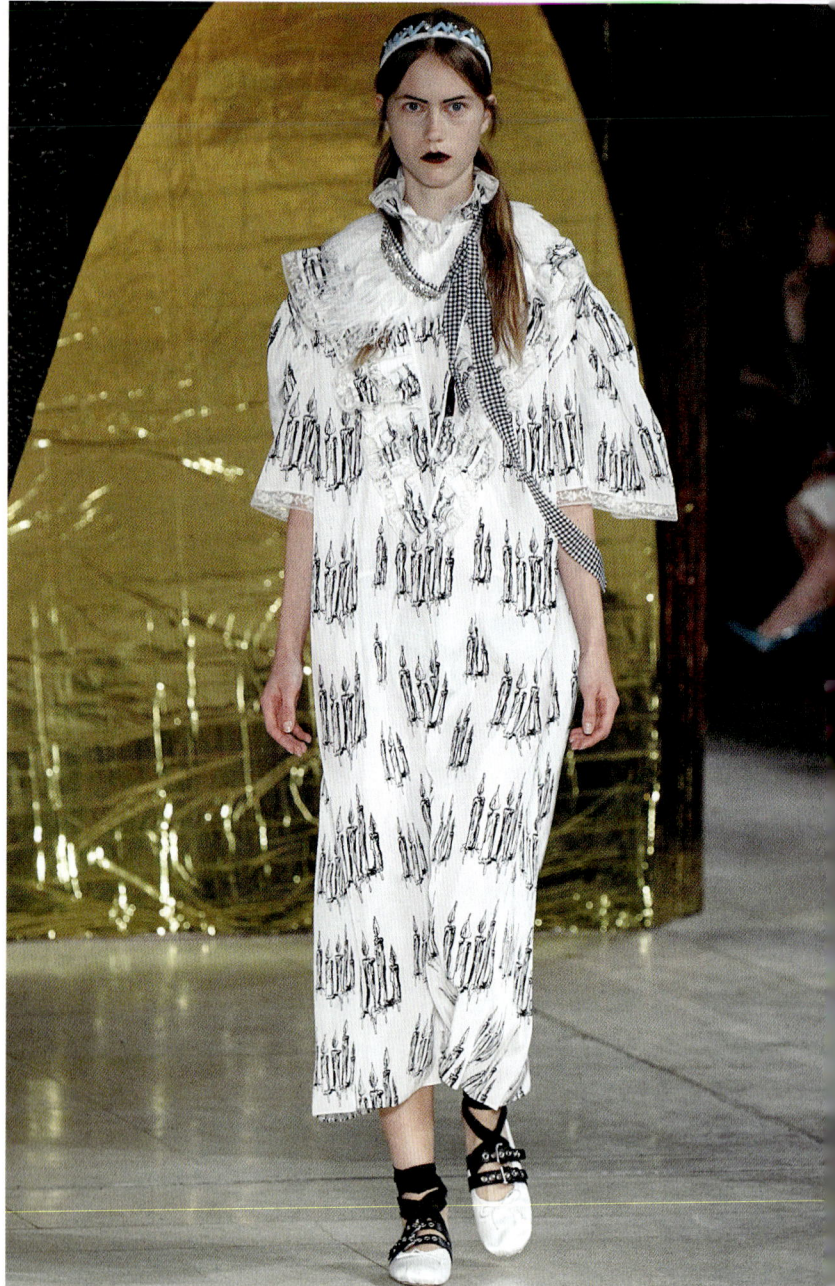

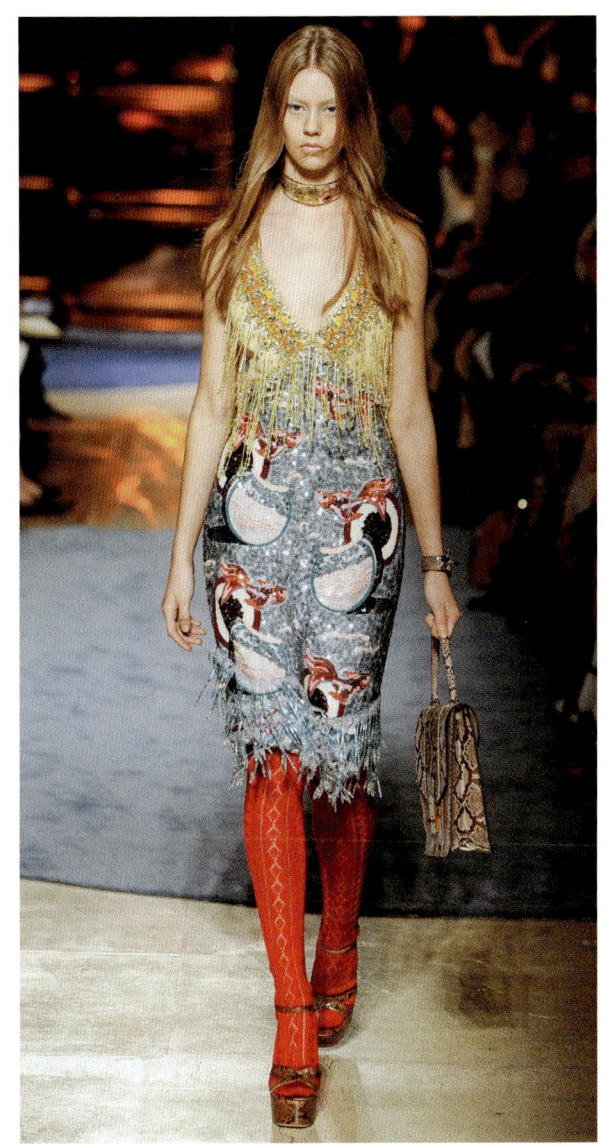

RIGHT The Spring/ Summer 2014 collection was full of prints done in collaboration with the artist Jeanne Detallante.

OPPOSITE Artist Eri Wakiyama designed the candle print seen here for Spring/ Summer 2016.

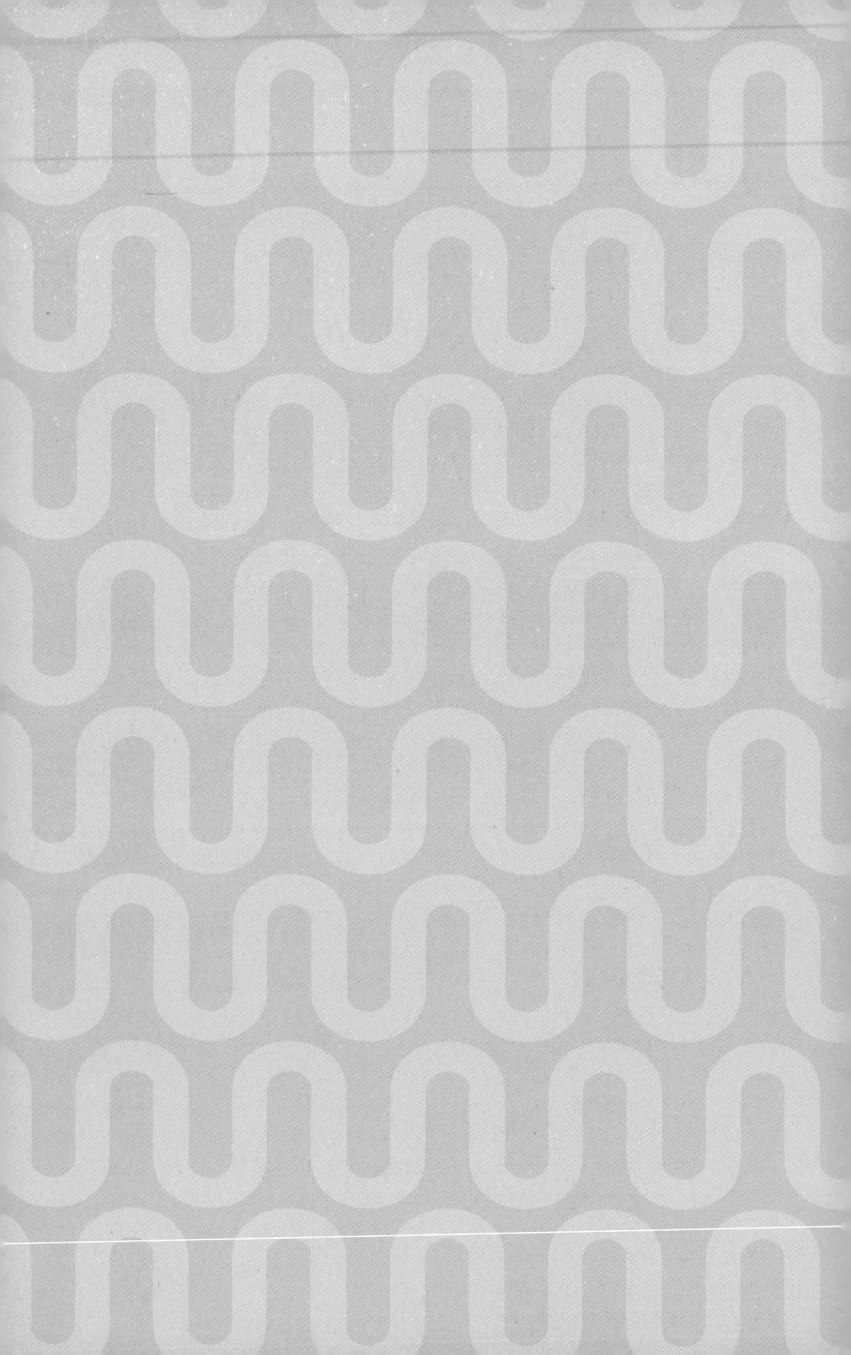

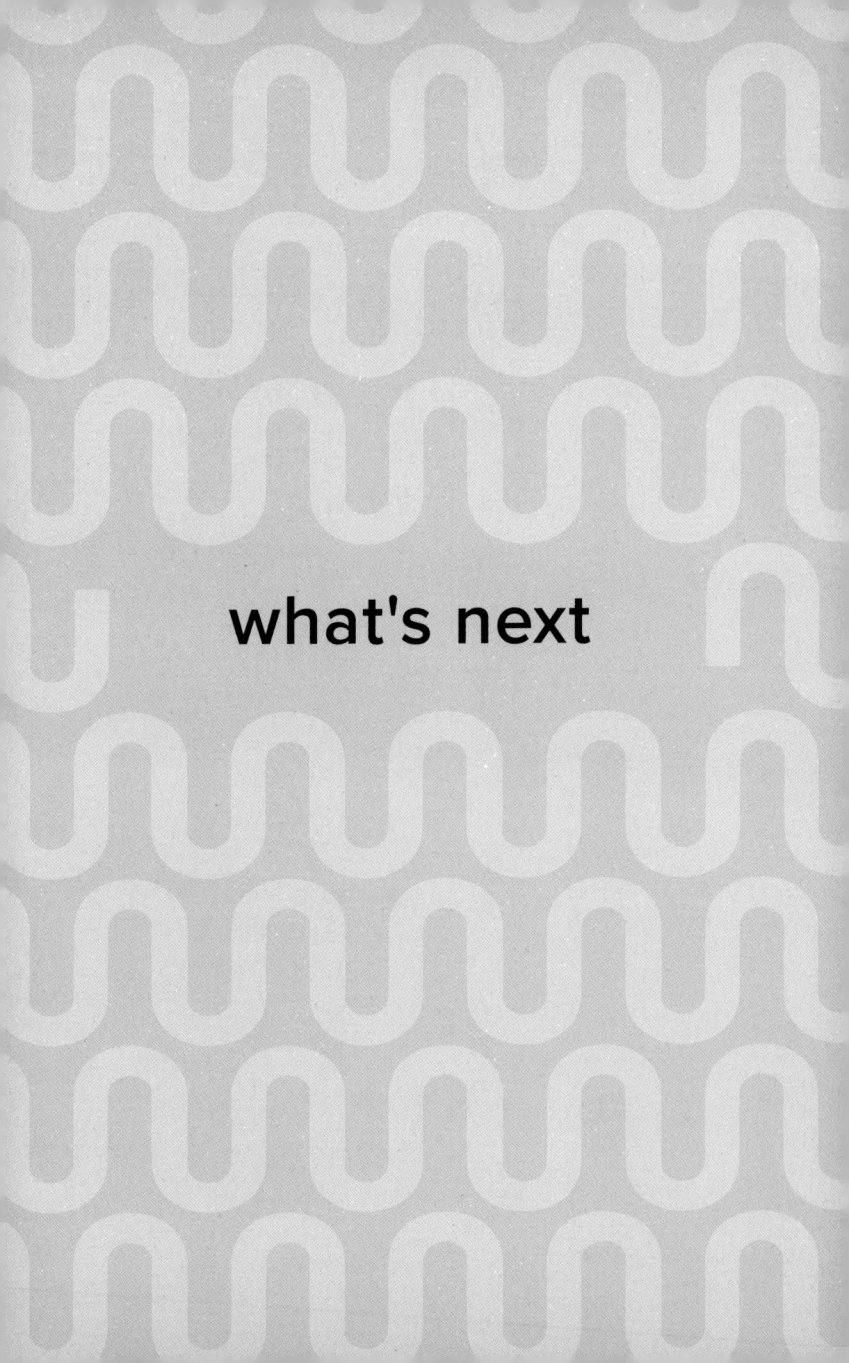

what's next

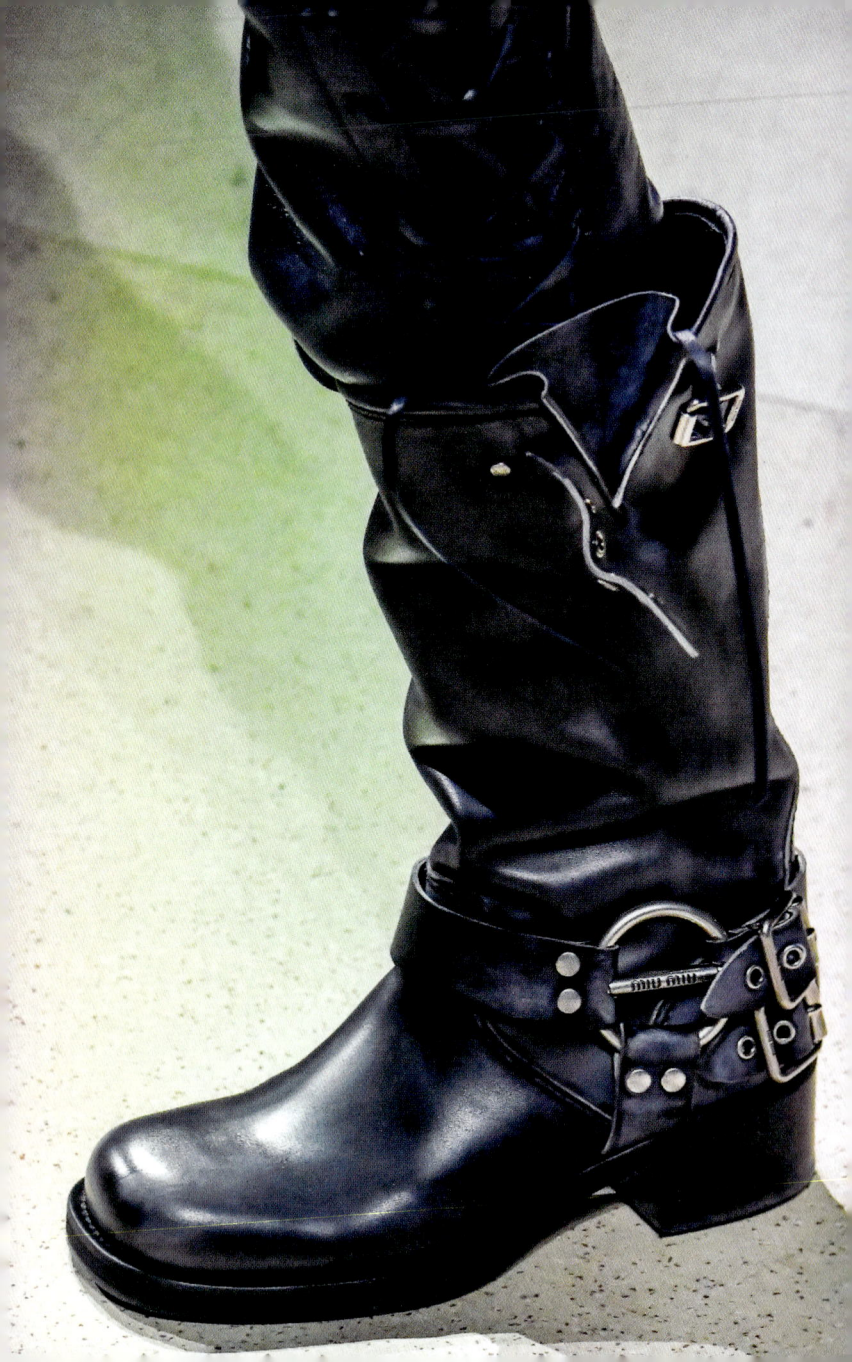

the future of
miu miu

Miuccia Prada once told *T* magazine that, "Clothes were never about doing clothes." Rather, "It's about living different parts of your personality." And so, it comes as no surprise that Miu Miu will probably always be associated with a strong point of view.

I n February 2020, the legendary Belgian designer Raf Simons joined Prada as the co-creative director. Simons worked a brief stint at Prada before leading Jil Sander, Dior and Calvin Klein, as well as his own namesake brand. Now jointly responsible for designing Prada's women's and men's wear, some of the most dedicated fans of the brand have noticed a more directional shift towards minimalism – such as fewer prints, not as much embellishment and more of Simons doing what Simons does, which is lots of fluid minimalism, oversized shapes, bomber jackets and a nod to uniform dressing. For the time being, Miuccia Prada is still solely responsible for Miu Miu, and Simons reportedly doesn't touch the brand. Still, she has often said that Miu Miu and Prada go hand in hand, and it's impossible not to notice a more minimal leaning at Miu Miu almost as soon as Simons joined.

OPPOSITE Miu Miu's footwear remains covetable, particularly utilitarian styles like the biker boots.

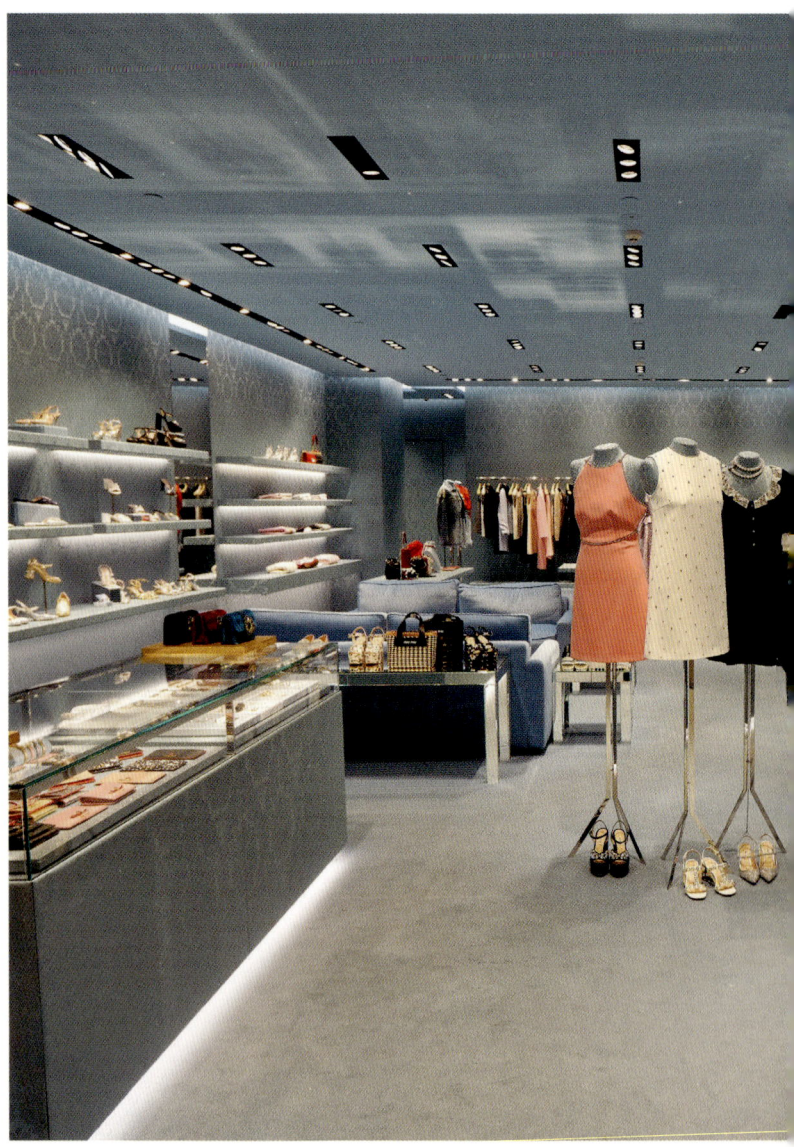

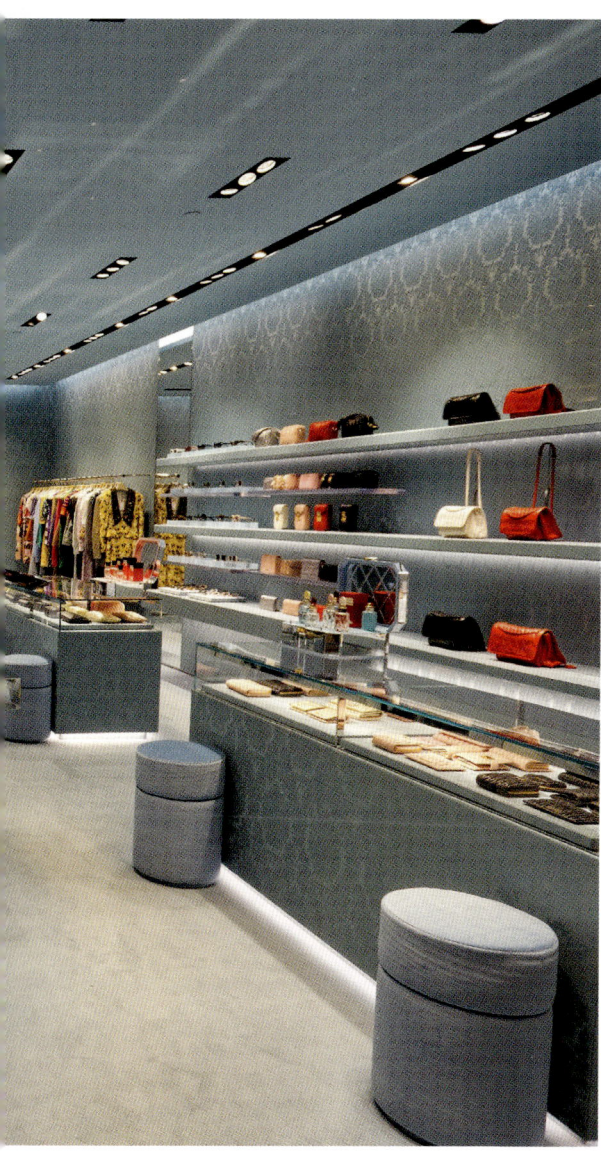

LEFT Miu Miu stores are recognized globally for their clean, feminine interiors.

In January 2024, Miuccia Prada and her husband, Bertelli, 76, stepped down as co-CEOs of Prada Group and appointed the former CEO of Luxottica Group, Andrea Guerra, in their place. According to the duo, they eventually plan to hand over the company to their eldest son, Lorenzo. "I decided that I didn't want to tell stories anymore," Miuccia Prada told *T* magazine in 2023. "We'll see how long it lasts."

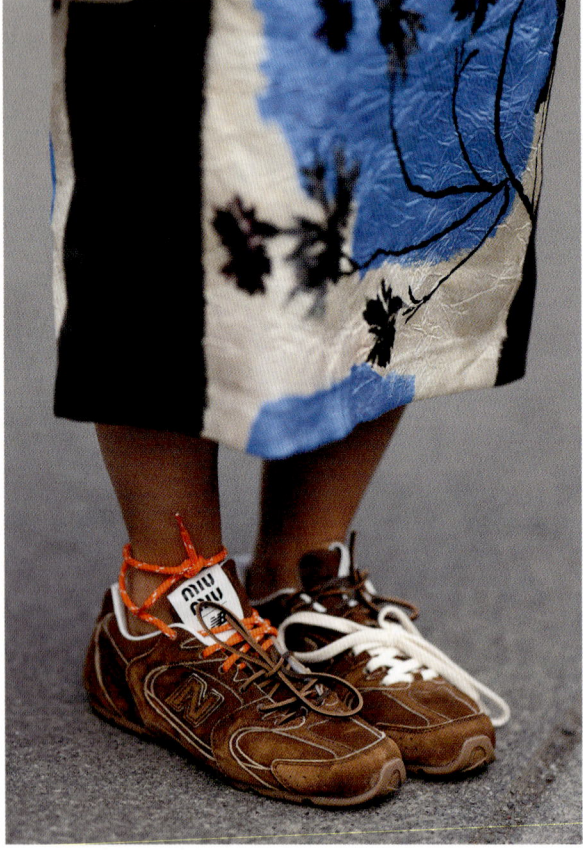

LEFT Miu Miu continues to pump out collaborations and It items that instantly sell out, such as the New Balance sneakers.

Miu Miu Beauty

Even after a pandemic and a luxury slowdown, the brand shows no signs of stopping.

In the first quarter of 2024, sales rose 89 per cent year on year. Likewise, retail sales were up 58 per cent in 2023. Miu Miu's explosive growth kicked off in 2021, after the micro miniskirt had its viral moment. Lyst, the well-respected fashion data tool and shopping app, named Miu Miu the Brand of the Year in both 2022 and 2023, highlighting the micro miniskirt, the celebrity front-row guests and the overall collections themselves as big conversation-drivers. Miu Miu's sneakers collaboration with New Balance, tiny swim briefs and polo top were also on the shopping platform's list of the top 10 hottest products from the period. In 2015, Miu Miu started selling its first perfume with Coty, later developing a series of different scents under its portfolio. The brand also recently expanded its beauty line, inking a deal with L'Oréal for the exclusive worldwide licensing agreement.

BELOW Miu Miu's perfumes touch on some of the same themes as the clothing line, such as femininity and expressiveness.

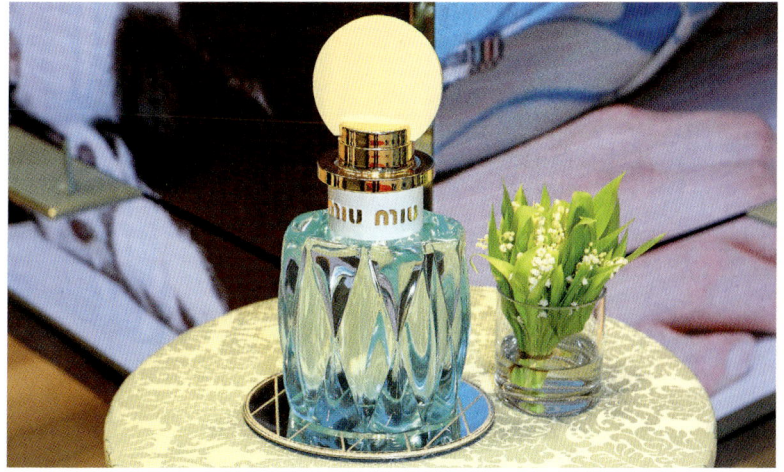

Miu Miu Menswear and Vintage Revival

There's also been a revival of interest in Miu Miu menswear. Even if Miu Miu has experimented by putting gender-fluid looks on the runway and sprinkling in bits of menswear to recent womenswear collections, fans are craving the originals. As the line was produced only from 1999 to 2008, pieces on the secondhand market are harder to find than vintage Miu Miu womenswear. In 2023, a *Vogue* article was titled: "Why Fashion Archivists Are Obsessed With Miu Miu Men's". Most fans love that the brand was so early in its approach to gender-fluid dressing, mirroring Miu Miu's womenswear but also having its own unique point of view. Some of the rarest pieces are from the earliest times Miu Miu did menswear – like the Spring/Summer 1999 and Autumn/Winter 1999 collections.

Luckily, for the biggest Miu Miu menswear fans, the brand has brought it back in small doses. The Spring/Summer 2022 collection introduced a few menswear looks alongside the regular womenswear pieces such as pleated micro miniskirts, crystal chain link dresses and oversized blazers. Many of the models were gender-fluid and many of the looks could be worn by anyone. Here, male models wore tight burgundy leather pants, Argyle sweaters, polo shirts and shorts. In subsequent runway collections, Miu Miu has integrated pieces that are both unisex and clearly designed for men, albeit in very small doses, as in a handful of looks per collection. For the Spring/Summer 2024 show, the iconic singer Troye Sivan walked the runway in a Miu Miu menswear look consisting of a polo shirt with a button-down shirt layered underneath it and silky knee-length shorts. If the demand is any indication, Miu Miu menswear is going to keep coming. These days, there's been more demand than ever before for rare Miu Miu pieces of the past. People collect and hoard pieces

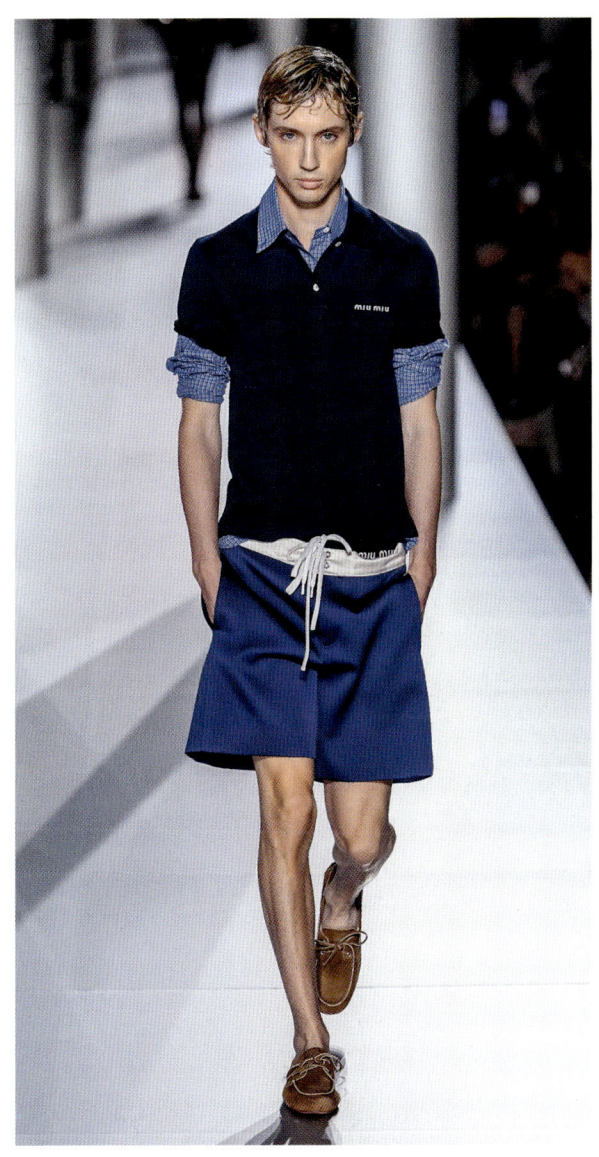

RIGHT In 2023, the singer-songwriter and actor Troye Sivan walked the runway for Miu Miu.

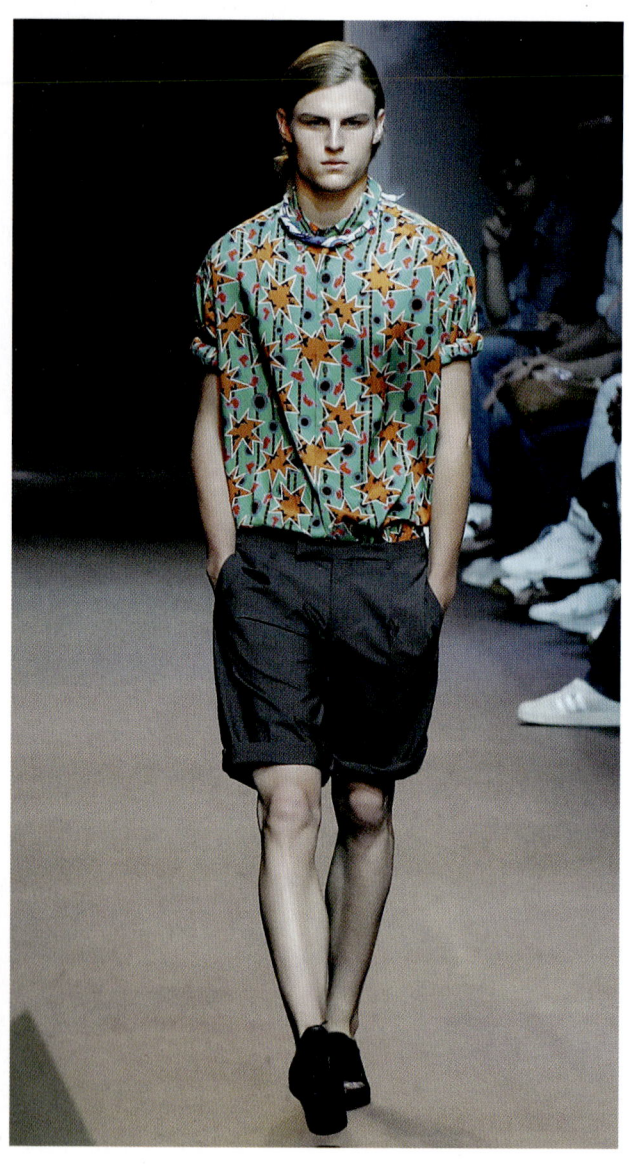

LEFT Miu Miu
menswear is still
popular even if
the line is defunct
and fans of the
brand still search
for pieces, as
seen here, on
the second-hand
market.

OPPOSITE The
accessories
from Miu Miu's
maximalist era are
also still popular
with fans.

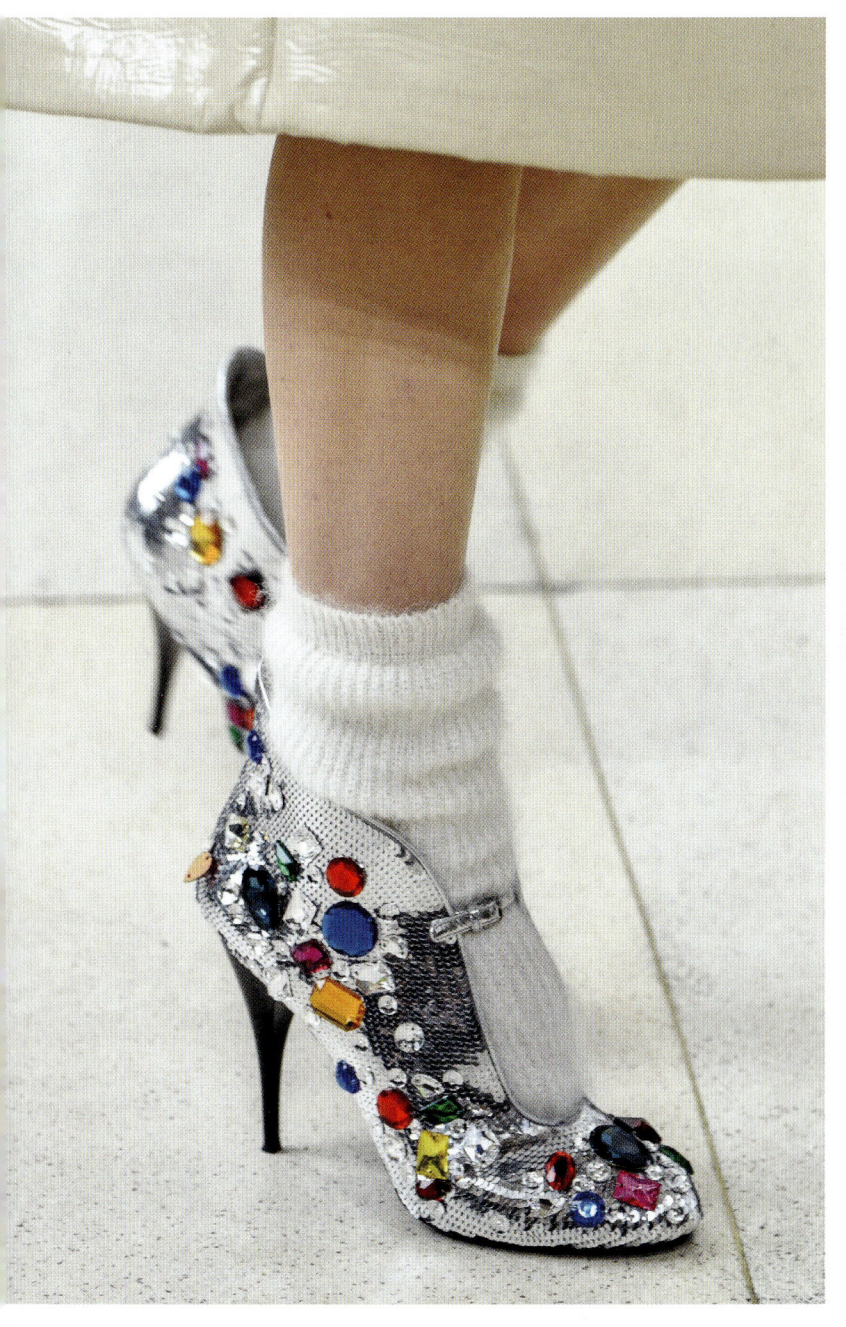

from the early collections. In particular, the shoes, which have a very ugly chic, utilitarian feel, with bubble soles, square toes and neutral hues. Compared to other designer vintage fashion, these pieces are relatively easy to find and less expensive than others.

The early Miu Miu bags, which can be described as fashionably sporty, are also in high demand. And with much of the recent designs going back to the roots of minimalism, there's been a revival in demand for maximalist Miu Miu holy grails. It's rare to find a Miu Miu coat covered in prints and excessive embellishment right now, but the pendulum constantly swings, so that may very well change. With superfans missing that over-the-top look from the mid 2010s, pieces from that era go very quickly on the secondhand market. For the biggest fans of Miu Miu, that indelible perspective of womanhood and girlhood – combined with cutting-edge, thought-provoking style – is what keeps everyone coming back time and time again.

RIGHT Miu Miu shoes from the mid-2010s, such as these strappy wedges, are instantly recognizable for their quirks.

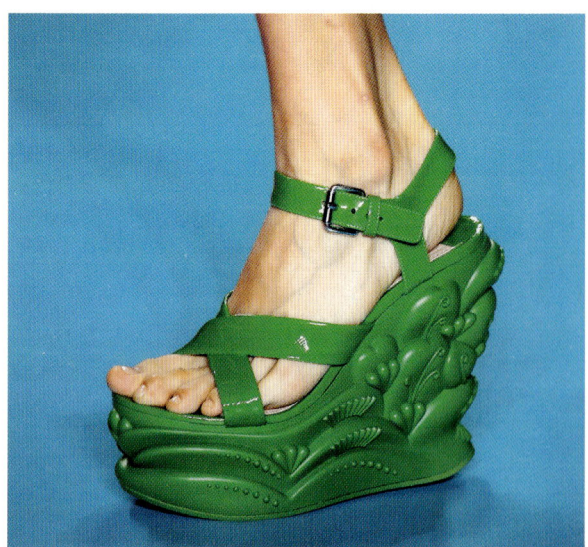

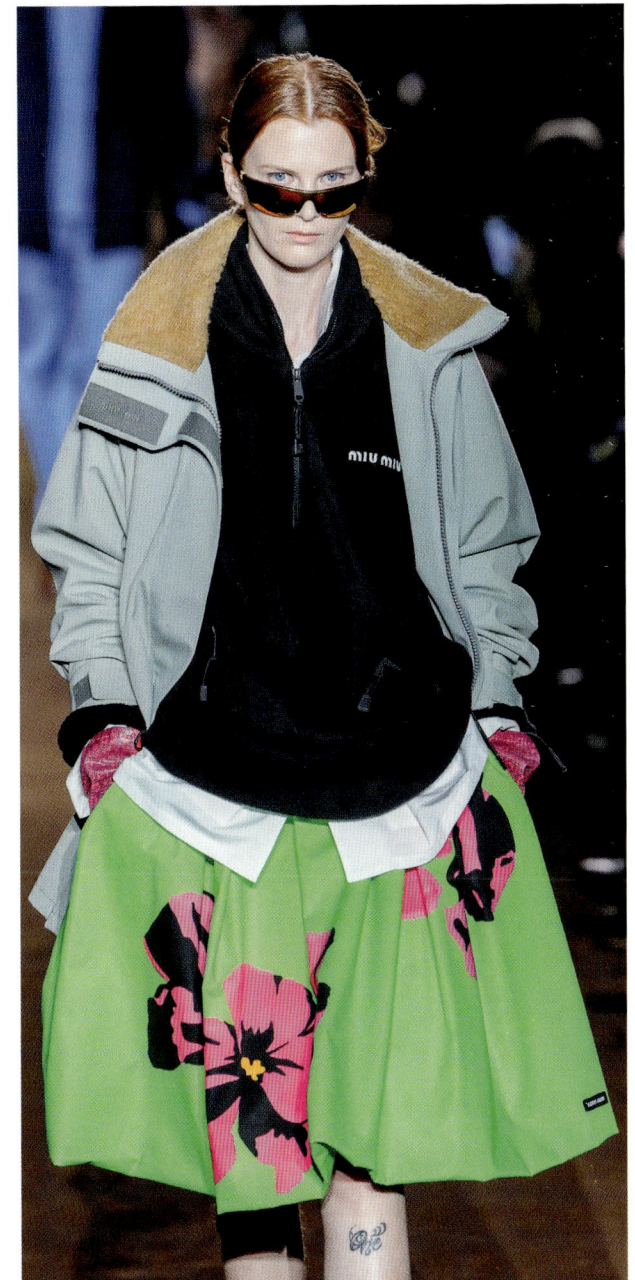

RIGHT The Autumn/Winter 2024 collection touched on quirky Miu Miu colours and prints, with cool, tomboyish styling.

index

credits

The publishers would like to thank the following sources for their kind permission to reproduce the pictures in this book.

Alamy Stock Photo: AP Photo/Luca Bruno 36; /Blanca Saenz de Castillo 137

Getty Images: Bryan Bedder/Getty Images for Miu Miu 144; /Dave Benett/Getty Images for Miu Miu 149; /Victor Boyko 44-45, 68, 125, 155; /Victor Boyko/Getty Images for Miu Miu 104, 107, 134; /Gareth Cattermole 124; /Dominique Charriau/WireImage 113; /George Chinsee/WWD via Getty Images 115; /Timothy Clary/AFP via Getty Images 53, 64; /Estrop 6, 47, 94, 97, 103, 154; /Fairchild Archive/Alain Jocard/AFP via Getty Images 9; /Fairchild Archive/Penske Media via Getty Images 71, 76, 78, 82, 128, 141; /Giovanni Giannoni/Penske Media via Getty Images 31, 42-43, 55, 63, 85, 138; /Gotham 117; /Francois Guillot/AFP via Getty Images 75; /Rose Hartman 20; /Taylor Hill 48; /Thomas Iannaccone/Penske Media via Getty Images 24; /Patrick Kovarik/AFP via Getty Images 79 80-81; /Pascal Le Segretain 87-88, 123; /Davide Maestri/Penske Media via Getty Images 25, 26, 70; /Dominique Maître/WWD/Penske Media via Getty Images 29, 86, 151; /Patrick McMullan via Getty Images 110; /Robert Mitra/Penske Media 22, 23 via Getty Images; /Jeremy Moeller 148; /Antonio de Moraes Barros Filho/WireImage 51, 100; /Penske Media via Getty Images 8; /Bertrand Rindoff Petroff 64-65; /David Prutting/Patrick McMullan via Getty Images 77; /Julien De Rosa/AFP via Getty Images 130-131; /Paco Serinelli/AFP via Getty Images 32-33, 152; /Art Streiber/WWD/Penske Media via Getty Images 14, 16-17, 18, 19; /Pierre Verdy/AFP via Getty Images 35, 37, 40, 57, 72; /Victor Virgile/Gamma-Rapho via Getty Images 27, 58, 60, 62, 83, 91, 96, 99, 118, 121, 122, 133, 140, 144; /Ricky Vigil M/GC Images 112; /Peter White 153

Shutterstock: 50; /Sorbis 145-146; /Marcy Swingle 93

Kristen Bateman is a New York based writer, editor, designer and consultant. She is the author of five books, including *Fashion's Big Night Out: The Met Gala Look Book*, *The Little Book of New York Style* and *Interior Style: Maximalism*. Her writing has appeared in the *New York Times*, *Vogue*, *Harper's Bazaar*, *W*, *Elle* and more. She is an avid fashion collector, and she also runs her own jewelry brand, Dollchunk. Follow along @kristenvbateman.